COOKING WITH
Bon Appétit

COOKING WITH
Bon Appétit

Make-Ahead Meals

THE KNAPP PRESS
Publishers
Los Angeles

Copyright © 1982 by Knapp Communications Corporation

Published by The Knapp Press
5900 Wilshire Boulevard, Los Angeles, California 90036

Library of Congress Cataloging in Publication Data

Main entry under title:

Cooking with Bon appétit.

    Includes index.
    1. Cookery I. Bon appétit. II. Title:
Make-ahead meals.
TX652.C736 1982   641.5′55   82-13097
ISBN 0-89535-106-4

On the cover: *Chicken and Corn Pot Pie*

Printed and bound in the United States of America

10 9 8 7 6 5 4 3 2

🍎 Contents

Foreword . . . . *vii*

1 Appetizers *1*

2 Soups 13

3 Salads 25

4 Entrées 33

    Seafood 34
    Poultry 42
    Pork 47
    Beef and Veal 52
    Lamb 59
    Game 62
    Vegetables, Cheese and Pasta 64

5 Accompaniments 69

    Vegetables 70
    Condiments, Pickles and Preserves 75
    Breads and Pastries 82

6 *Desserts* *93*

    Fruit *94*

    Custards and Creams *95*

    Cakes and Pastries *98*

    Cookies *106*

    Frozen Desserts and Sauces *110*

Index *115*

❦ *Foreword*

For those of us who love to cook but lead busy lives, preparing exciting, delicious food every day is a constant challenge. Often, we simply cannot spare the time to cook an entire meal in one kitchen session from start to finish. As with any creative pastime, we tend to reserve our serious cooking for weekends or the occasional free evening.

Some of that time is well spent cooking dishes we can continue to enjoy for days, weeks or even months to come. At *Bon Appétit*, we always try to offer our readers hints on how to prepare recipes in advance and how to store them for future enjoyment. All kinds of excellent dishes can be cooked ahead of time and kept with the certainty that they will stay as good as they were when freshly made—or even improve in flavor. Still other recipes can be prepared at least partly in advance: a sauce whipped up, meat or vegetables sliced, pastry rolled out and trimmed, all ready for the final cooking or assembly of the dish.

On the following pages you will find more than 200 of the best make-ahead recipes from the pages of *Bon Appétit*. For your ease in menu planning, they are divided into six chapters by the roles they play in a meal, from appetizers to desserts. Each chapter also includes informative features on key aspects of make-ahead cooking. Guidelines for freezing foods, for example, are given on pages 8–9 of the first chapter. In the section on soups you will find recipes for basic stocks of meat or fish (pages 18–19), invaluable assets that can be prepared in quantity and are easily stored in the freezer. And the chapter on accompaniments and side dishes includes hints on bottling herb-flavored vinegars (page 77), dealing with croissant dough (page 87) and mixing and storing pastry doughs (page 90).

With the aid of such information, and with some careful selection and planning, you could, if you like, compose an entire menu from dishes made in advance. But one make-ahead recipe alone will give special flair to a meal. A robust Chicken and Corn Pot Pie (see cover; recipe, page 46), for example, needs only a tossed green salad and some bread for a wholesome family dinner. Danish pastries (page 86), prepared the night before and popped into the oven to bake the next morning, give distinction to any breakfast or brunch. Even the simple touch of a tangy condiment or pickle, opened and served in a matter of seconds, will speak of hours spent making good things in the kitchen.

1 ❦ Appetizers

As the saying goes, first impressions always count. Appetizers set the tone for the meal to come, and they deserve special attention from the cook. But special attention need not mean special effort—particularly when so many appetizers can be prepared partly or entirely in advance.

Most spreads and dips, for example, are whipped up in a matter of seconds; once made, they store well in the refrigerator. All you need do to complete the presentation is to add a crusty loaf, some specialty breads like thinly sliced pumpernickel, crackers, fresh vegetables cut into "crudités" or—in the case of the light, creamy Gorgonzola with Madeira spread on page 10—pieces of cool, fresh fruit. More formal occasions may call for a little extra advance preparation: the Terrine Maison on page 4, a pistachio-studded mixture of chicken liver, ground beef and ground veal, benefits from being prepared as much as four days ahead, to allow time for its flavors to mellow.

Pastry-based appetizers, from cheese-filled phyllo turnovers (page 10) to chou pastry Herbed Gougères (page 7) to Chinese-style Sausage-Spinach Buns (page 11), are real assets for make-ahead cooking. They freeze superbly, and can be stored for months. If they were baked before freezing, all they need is gentle reheating; pastries frozen unbaked require just a few minutes of extra cooking time.

In choosing an appetizer, it is wise to give careful consideration to the rest of the menu, with an eye to pleasing contrasts or counterpoints to the main course. A simple seafood entrée, for example, is best preceded by a light vegetable or cheese appetizer. Heartier main courses can sustain more complex or strongly flavored hors d'oeuvres. If you start with an appetizer whose flavors will not be repeated later in the meal, your menu will offer fresh delights from first course to last.

Belgian Endive with Yogurt Dipping Sauce

The dip can be prepared two or three days ahead, the platter assembled the morning before serving and refrigerated. Put the dip in a small white bowl set on a white plate, then arrange the endive leaves in layers like chrysanthemum petals.

12 servings

2 cups plain yogurt
2 shallots, coarsely chopped
1 teaspoon dry basil or 1 tablespoon fresh basil, chopped
¼ teaspoon dry marjoram or ¾ teaspoon fresh marjoram, chopped

1 teaspoon dry chervil or 1 tablespoon fresh chervil, chopped
Dash of Worchestershire sauce
Salt and freshly ground papper

4 heads Belgian endive

Combine all ingredients except endive in food processor or blender and blend until smooth. Refrigerate 2 to 3 days.

Morning before serving, separate and rinse endive leaves and assemble platter. Reserve some dip for refills. Cover platter with plastic wrap and chill.

Chick-Pea Spread (Hummus)

Hummus can be prepared up to two days ahead. Refrigerate until ready to serve.

4 to 6 servings

1 cup dried chick-peas, rinsed and drained
½ cup tahini (sesame seed paste)*
½ cup fresh lemon juice
¼ cup plain yogurt mixed with ¼ cup water
¼ cup minced fresh parsley

2 tablespoons tamari soy sauce
2 green onions, minced (green tops included)
2 garlic cloves, minced
1 tablespoon virgin olive oil
½ teaspoon ground cumin
⅛ teaspoon honey

Combine chick-peas in large saucepan with enough water to cover and let mixture soak overnight.

Drain chick-peas well; add fresh water to cover. Place over high heat and bring to boil. Reduce heat to medium and boil gently until chick-peas are very tender, about 2½ to 3 hours. Drain and let cool. Remove skins. Transfer chick-peas to processor or blender and puree until smooth.

Transfer puree to medium bowl. Stir in remaining ingredients. Taste and adjust seasoning as desired.

Serve with warm whole wheat pita bread.

*Tahini is available in natural foods stores and in Middle Eastern markets.

Eggplant and Sesame Spread (Baba Ghanouj)

This spread can be prepared one day ahead.

4 to 6 servings

1 large eggplant
½ cup tahini (sesame seed paste)*
¼ cup (or more) fresh lemon juice
4 green onions, minced (including green tops)
3 to 4 garlic cloves, crushed
3 tablespoons toasted sesame seed
2 tablespoons plus 1 teaspoon virgin olive oil

2 tablespoons minced fresh parsley
1 tablespoon tamari soy sauce
⅛ teaspoon honey
Pinch of ground red pepper
Freshly ground pepper

Chopped fresh parsley (garnish)

Preheat oven to 450°F. Make several cuts in eggplant with sharp knife. Combine eggplant in large saucepan with enough salted water to cover completely. Weight with smaller saucepan filled with water and let soak 20 minutes. Rinse under cold water. Transfer to baking sheet and roast, turning occasionally, until eggplant is very soft, about 50 to 60 minutes. Let cool; peel and seed eggplant. Transfer pulp to small bowl and mash with fork, or transfer to blender and puree (eggplant should retain some texture).

Combine tahini and ¼ cup lemon juice in large bowl and mix well. Add more lemon juice if necessary to make thick paste. Add green onion, garlic, sesame seed, 2 tablespoons oil, parsley, soy sauce, honey, ground red pepper and pepper and mix well. Stir in eggplant puree. Adjust seasoning.

Transfer mixture to shallow serving dish, spreading evenly to edges. Drizzle with remaining 1 teaspoon olive oil and sprinkle with chopped parsley. Refrigerate until ready to serve.

*Tahini is available in natural foods stores and in Middle Eastern markets.

Guacamole with Ground Beef

The ground beef can be prepared up to two days ahead and refrigerated, then reheated just before guacamole ingredients are added.

8 servings

2 tablespoons oil
1 large onion, minced
1 pound lean ground beef
1 teaspoon ground cumin
½ teaspoon crumbled dry oregano or 1½ teaspoons minced fresh oregano
¼ teaspoon cayenne pepper or to taste
⅛ teaspoon ground coriander

Pinch of whole caraway seed
1 large garlic clove, minced
Salt and freshly ground pepper

2 large ripe avocados, peeled, seeded and finely chopped
1 cup sour cream
¼ cup mayonnaise
Juice of ½ lemon
Taco chips

Heat oil in large heavy skillet over medium-high heat. Add onion and sauté until soft. Increase heat to high, add beef and cook until browned. Stir in seasonings and garlic. Cook another minute, stirring constantly. Season to taste with salt and pepper. Drain off all fat. Turn into large bowl. *(Can be refrigerated up to 2 days at this point. Reheat before adding remaining ingredients.)*

Add next 4 ingredients and toss lightly. Taste and adjust seasoning. Serve immediately with taco chips.

Duxelles Canapés

Duxelles topping can be prepared several days in advance. Canapés can be assembled the day before and refrigerated.

Makes 4 dozen

2 tablespoons olive oil
2 tablespoons minced shallot or white part of green onion
1 pound mushrooms, minced
¼ cup Madeira
½ cup whipping cream
2 ounces cream cheese, crumbled
1 egg yolk, room temperature
2 tablespoons minced prosciutto or other ham
1 tablespoon fresh lemon juice

¾ teaspoon fresh thyme, minced, or ¼ teaspoon dried, crumbled
Salt and freshly ground pepper
⅛ teaspoon freshly grated nutmeg
4 tablespoons freshly grated Parmesan cheese

24 pieces very thinly sliced firm white bread

Parsley sprigs (optional garnish)

Heat oil in heavy large skillet over low heat. Add shallot and stir constantly until translucent. Add mushrooms and cook over low heat until mushrooms become dark in color and begin to separate into small individual pieces, about 20 minutes; stir often to prevent sticking. Add Madeira and continue cooking over low heat until it evaporates, approximately 1 hour. Add cream and cook until absorbed. Add cream cheese and stir until melted. Stir in egg yolk, prosciutto, lemon juice, thyme, salt, pepper, nutmeg and 1 tablespoon of the Parmesan cheese.

Cut out 48 crustless canapés from bread with 1½-inch fluted cutter and arrange on baking sheet. Divide duxelles topping among canapés. Sprinkle with remaining 3 tablespoons Parmesan.

Just before serving, preheat oven to 400°F. Bake canapés until brown, about 10 minutes. Garnish each with small parsley sprig, if desired.

Chicken and Tuna Terrine

Terrine can be made three days ahead.

2 servings

1 slice firm-textured white bread (crusts trimmed), torn into pieces
½ cup milk
1 whole chicken breast, skinned, boned and cut into chunks (about 10 ounces boned)
1 3¼-ounce can tuna, well drained
1 1-ounce can anchovy fillets, drained
¼ cup chopped fresh parsley

1 egg
1 tablespoon capers, rinsed and drained
½ onion, diced
1 garlic clove, minced
Juice and peel of 1 lemon

Lemon slices and sliced black olives (garnish)

Preheat oven to 350°F. Combine bread and milk in small bowl and let soak 5 minutes. Squeeze bread dry; discard milk. Transfer bread to processor or blender. Add chicken, tuna, 2 anchovy fillets, parsley, egg, capers, onion, garlic, lemon juice and peel and mix until smooth, scraping down sides of container several times (if using blender, puree mixture in batches).

Butter 6 × 3 × 2¼-inch loaf pan. Arrange remaining anchovies in lattice pattern in bottom. Spoon tuna mixture into pan, smoothing top. Set in another pan containing 1 inch boiling water. Bake until set, 40 to 50 minutes. Remove terrine from water bath and let cool. Drain any liquid from terrine. Wrap in foil and refrigerate overnight. Unmold onto platter and garnish with lemon and olives. Serve with French bread and a homemade caper-laced mayonnaise.

Terrine Maison with Cumberland Sauce

Terrine can be made up to four days ahead.

8 to 10 servings

1 pound sliced bacon, blanched
1½ pounds chicken livers, ground
1 pound lean ground beef
1 pound lean ground veal
1 cup whipping cream
6 eggs
2 teaspoons salt
2 teaspoons freshly ground pepper
1 teaspoon freshly grated nutmeg

½ cup brandy
1 cup shelled pistachio nuts

6 whole chicken livers
6 strips uncooked bacon
6 slices boiled ham

Cumberland Sauce (see following recipe)

Line 12 × 3 × 3-inch loaf pan with overlapping strips of bacon. Refrigerate.

Combine ground liver, beef and veal in processor and mix well. Transfer to mixing bowl. Add cream, eggs, salt, pepper and nutmeg. Warm brandy, ignite and add to bowl. Mix in nuts.

Spread half of pâté in loaf pan. Wrap each whole liver in a strip of bacon and arrange down center of pan. Cut ham into strips and use to fill in spaces between bacon-wrapped livers. Spread remaining pâté evenly over top. Cover with overlapping bacon strips.

Preheat oven to 350°F. Double a piece of heavy-duty foil and cover top of terrine. Set pan in larger shallow pan and fill with water to depth of 1 inch. Bake 2 hours. Remove terrine from water bath, uncover and continue baking until juices are no longer rosy (or until meat thermometer inserted in center registers 170°F to 175°F), about 30 minutes. Remove from oven and carefully pour off excess liquid. Let cool completely. Set in refrigerator, place baking sheet on top and weight entire surface with bricks or heavy cans. Chill thoroughly before unmolding. Serve with Cumberland Sauce over top.

Cumberland Sauce

Makes about 1⅓ cups

5 **shallots, finely chopped**	½ **cup currant jelly**
Peel and juice of 1 orange (cut peel julienne)	½ **cup Port**
	1 **teaspoon Dijon mustard**
Peel and juice of 1 lemon (cut peel julienne)	**Pinch of ground ginger**
	Pinch of ground red pepper

Combine shallots, citrus peel and juice in small saucepan. Place over low heat and simmer 10 minutes, stirring frequently. Add remaining ingredients and simmer 10 minutes, stirring occasionally. Serve at room temperature.

Pâté en Croûte

A delicious party spread that can be made ahead and frozen up to two weeks. Accompany with Melba toast, cornichons or pickled cherries.

Makes 3 cups

3 **cups (6 sticks) unsalted butter, room temperature**	1 **tablespoon fresh lemon juice**
3 **large onions, sliced**	1½ **to 2 teaspoons salt**
¾ **cup sliced shallot or white part of green onion**	¾ **to 1½ teaspoons quatre épices, optional**
1 **cup peeled and chopped green apples**	¾ **teaspoon freshly ground pepper**
3 **pounds chicken livers, halved**	**Basic Short Pastry dough (see recipe, page 91)**
¾ **cup Cognac**	

Melt 9 tablespoons (1 stick plus 1 tablespoon) butter in large skillet over medium heat. Add sliced onion and shallot and sauté until golden brown. Add apples and cook until soft enough to mash with back of spoon, about 5 minutes. Transfer to bowl and set aside. *Do not clean the skillet.*

Melt 9 more tablespoons butter in same skillet over medium-high heat. Add chicken livers in batches and sauté until browned on outside but still pink inside. Return all livers to skillet, remove from heat and flame with Cognac.

Combine livers and apple mixture in batches in processor or blender and puree until smooth. Transfer to bowl and let cool. Cover and chill well.

Cream remaining butter in large bowl until smooth. Gradually beat in pâté, blending well after each addition. Add all remaining ingredients except pastry and mix well. Adjust seasoning. Pack mixture into 3 8-ounce soufflé dishes or a 1-quart terrine. Cover *surface of pâté tightly* with plastic wrap. Refrigerate.

Preheat oven to 350°F. Roll out pastry on lightly floured board to thickness of ¼ inch. Cut into circle slightly larger than 1-quart terrine (or into 3 rounds if using soufflé dishes). Set round(s) on baking sheet, crimping edge(s) decoratively. Roll out scraps and shape into leaves, flower petals, etc. and set on top of round(s). Bake until golden. Cool completely on rack. Just before serving, remove plastic wrap from pâté and set pastry over terrine or soufflé dishes for decorative cap.

Vegetable Antipasto

A Genovese-style antipasto that makes use of seasonal vegetables, this can be prepared up to three days ahead and refrigerated.

12 servings

6 medium zucchini
6 crookneck squash
2 medium yellow onions

6 firm medium tomatoes
6 medium green peppers

5 tablespoons olive oil
½ onion, finely chopped

Olive oil
12 eggs, beaten
2 cups very fine dry breadcrumbs

2 cups freshly grated Parmesan cheese
2 teaspoons coarsely chopped fresh marjoram or ¾ teaspoon dried, crumbled
Salt and freshly ground pepper
Freshly grated nutmeg
Minced fresh parsley

Olive oil
Freshly grated Parmesan cheese

Parboil zucchini and crookneck squash in large amount of salted water until just tender. Remove from pot with slotted spoon and drain well. Refresh under cold running water and drain again. Add onions to same water and parboil until tender. Drain well; refresh under cold water and drain again.

Cut tomatoes in half and carefully scoop out pulp, leaving ¼-inch shell (do not pierce skin). Set pulp aside. Cut peppers in half and remove seeds. Halve zucchini and crookneck squash horizontally and scoop out pulp, leaving ¼-inch shell. Halve onions from root to top; remove centers, leaving thin shell.

Heat 5 tablespoons olive oil in large skillet over medium heat. Add finely chopped onion and sauté until lightly golden. Chop tomato, zucchini and crookneck squash pulp and centers from onion. Add to skillet and cook 10 minutes, stirring frequently. Transfer to large bowl and let cool.

Preheat oven to 325°F. Generously oil large shallow baking dish. Add eggs, breadcrumbs, cheese, marjoram, salt, pepper, nutmeg and parsley to vegetable mixture and blend thoroughly. Taste and adjust seasoning (mixture should be very highly seasoned).

Arrange vegetable shells in single layer in baking dish so sides do not touch. Divide breadcrumb mixture among shells. Bake until filling is set, about 15 to 20 minutes. Drizzle with olive oil and sprinkle with Parmesan. Broil until filling is lightly golden. Let cool in pan. Serve at cool room temperature.

Vegetables à la Grecque

Can be prepared ahead. Cool, then cover and refrigerate up to 48 hours.

Vegetables à la Grecque must be cooked at a rolling boil in order for oil and liquid to emulsify and thicken the sauce.

6 to 8 servings

¼ cup coriander seed
1 tablespoon whole peppercorns
4 branches thyme
3 bay leaves
3 to 4 parsley sprigs

1½ to 2 cups water (substitute chicken stock when preparing mushrooms, cucumbers or artichokes)
¼ cup dry white wine
2 tablespoons tomato paste
2 tablespoons fresh lemon juice

¼ cup vegetable oil
¼ cup olive oil
20 to 25 small boiling onions

Vegetables
2 pounds of any *one* of the following:
Mushrooms, quartered if large
Cucumbers, cut into short lengths and pared into olive shape
Zucchini, cut into thick slices
Cauliflower, separated into florets
Cabbage, ribs only (save leaves for another use)
Green beans, ends removed
Artichoke bottoms, rubbed with cut lemon and sliced into 6 pieces

4 medium tomatoes, peeled, seeded   2 teaspoons salt
   and coarsely chopped

Combine coriander, peppercorns, thyme, bay leaves and parsley sprigs and tie in
cheesecloth bag; set aside.

Combine water or stock, wine, tomato paste and lemon juice; set aside.

Heat oils in large stockpot until haze forms. Add onions and sauté until lightly
browned, about 3 minutes. Add vegetable (see preceding list), chopped tomatoes,
salt, spice bag and tomato paste mixture. *(There should be enough liquid barely
to cover vegetables; add more water or stock if necessary.)*

Bring to rapid boil and boil hard until vegetables are tender. Allow about 9
minutes for mushrooms, cucumber and zucchini; about 15 minutes for cauliflower, cabbage and beans; about 20 to 25 minutes for artichoke bottoms.

Discard spice bag. Taste for seasoning; vegetables should be highly seasoned.
Serve at room temperature.

Herbed Gougères

*Even frozen and reheated
these puffs taste freshly
made. They have a springy
center and can be served
plain or filled with a small
pimiento-stuffed olive. The
basic gougère recipe, without the herbs and olives, is
the version served at the
three-star Taillevent restau-
rant in Paris.*

Makes 40 puffs

⅔ cup water
⅓ cup water
½ cup (1 stick) unsalted butter
1¼ teaspoons salt
½ teaspoon freshly grated nutmeg
     Freshly ground pepper
1 cup unbleached all purpose flour

5 eggs
2 tablespoons cold milk

4 ounces Gruyère cheese (rind
   removed), shredded (1 cup)
2 green onions (1 ounce total),
   minced
1 tablespoon minced parsley
1 teaspoon dried dillweed

½ teaspoon salt
40 small pimiento-stuffed olives
   (optional)

Position rack in center of oven. Preheat to 400°F. Butter 2 baking sheets.

Combine water, ⅓ cup milk, butter, salt, nutmeg and pepper in small saucepan and bring to boil over medium-high heat, making sure butter is completely
melted. Remove from heat and immediately stir in flour using wooden spoon until
all flour is absorbed and mixture leaves sides of pan. Return to medium heat 2
minutes to cook flour.

Transfer to mixing bowl. Beat in 4 eggs one at a time until mixture is thick
and smooth. Add milk and mix thoroughly. Blend in cheese, onion, parsley and
dill. (Batter should hold shape on a spoon.)

Lightly sprinkle prepared baking sheets with water, shaking off excess. Spoon
batter into 16-inch pastry bag fitted with ¾-inch tube. Pipe 1¼- to 1½-inch
mounds onto baking sheets.

Combine remaining egg and salt and blend well. Brush over tops of gougères,
being careful not to drip onto baking sheet or rising will be impaired. Bake until
well browned, about 20 to 25 minutes. Remove from baking sheets and cool on
wire racks. When cool, slit sides of puffs and insert olives.

*Cooled gougères (without olives) can be frozen in airtight plastic bags. Reheat
10 minutes in 300°F oven (do not preheat).*

🍒 Creative Freezing Guidelines

Planning

Develop a plan based on your family favorites and your own entertainment needs. Think of your freezer as a creative tool, not merely a storehouse for leftovers. Don't be a hoarder; keep the inventory changing.

Take a slow day to grate cheese, cook stock, toast croutons, chop onions or make a stack of crepes for freezing. When you get a good buy on mushrooms, make duxelles.

Freeze in meal-size quantities whether for family or bigger occasions. For meat, figure a quarter pound boned per person. If the meat has bones, allow half a pound per person. (Put extra freezer paper over the bone ends to prevent punctures in the wrapping.)

Keep an inventory; it will help you plan menus. If you have a big freezer, the list should also be a record of the contents of each section.

As part of your record-keeping, label every package you put in the freezer. With a felt-tip pen or wax pencil, note the contents and freezing date. You might want add "reheat at 375°F" or some other instruction.

Packaging

Take a minute to think about the best container for your purpose. Milk cartons are great for storing liquids such as stock, and their rectangular shape makes for easy stacking.

Save little plastic tubs for butters and odds and ends. Plastic bags work well for loose, bulky items like poultry stuffing, and they fit nicely into freezer crannies. The smaller the container, the faster the food will freeze and thaw. When you use gallon containers, fill halfway, cover with a double thickness of freezer paper, then fill the remaining half. For reheating, separate blocks.

Glass freezer jars, which have been tempered for hot and cold, work well, but avoid ordinary glass jars except in a pinch. Freezing makes them brittle.

For party quantities, use big disposable aluminum roasting pans which can go directly into the oven. Pie fillings can also be frozen in the containers in which they'll be baked. If you're short of pie plates and casseroles, freeze the food in the baking dish, then remove it when hard and wrap in plastic or freezer paper. When you're ready to reheat, slip it back into the dish.

Adequate wrapping is the key to successful freezing. All foods should have an airtight seal. Be sure contents are not hot when placed in bags or cartons, or they will stick together.

Take extra care with fish, sliced liver and veal. Wrap in plastic first, then in freezer foil to conserve flavor.

For large pieces of meat, like sirloin or chuck roast, put a thin coat of vegetable oil on the cut surface to seal in the juices and prevent freezer burn.

Wrap cakes in foil, plastic wrap, plastic bags or freezer paper. After they're hard, put them in strong cartons or in metal or plastic containers to avert squashing. To prevent damage to the top crust, cover a pie with a paper plate before wrapping. Store cookies in coffee or shortening cans.

Freezing and Defrosting

Flash (quick) freezing is preferred for pie shells and soft, small items to avoid crushing and save space. Place foods on a metal baking sheet without touching one another and set in the coldest section, freezing as quickly as possible. When solid, stack or scoop into a plastic bag or coffee can.

Don't freeze too much at a time. Crowding puts enough strain on the motor to render the freezer inefficient. Allow three to four pounds per cubic foot. Freezing takes from two to twenty-four hours, depending on the density of the food, package size and the amount to be frozen. Place packaged, cooled food in contact with the freezer surface. This speeds the process and minimizes flavor loss.

When you are preparing dishes specifically for freezing, undercook slightly. Reheating will bring them to their optimum state.

Do not refreeze food that has been cooked, frozen and reheated. A second reheating would overcook. In addition, as the food sits in the serving dish for a second time, then cools to go back to the freezer, bacteria can flourish.

When in doubt as to whether you may safely refreeze defrosted foods, here's a good rule to follow: Food that has been defrosted in the refrigerator and has not reached more than 40°F (ordinary refrigerator temperature) can safely be refrozen as long as color, odor and texture seem acceptable to you. This is a good thing to remember in case a power failure or other problems cause your freezer to break down.

Poultry or meat which has been frozen uncooked can be refrozen after cooking. Use refrozen foods as soon as possible. In general, a month's storage is safe for cooked foods. Soup stock as well as meat and poultry in liquid will last six months. Use sliced roasted meat and poultry within two weeks.

Shellfish spoil quickly after thawing. Since it's hard to detect spoilage either by odor or appearance, don't refreeze.

After you take things out of the freezer, you'll want to defrost some and cook others frozen. Don't defrost roasts before cooking. Instead, allow about twice the cooking time and cook at low temperature. After the meat has cooked enough to allow insertion of a thermometer, continue roasting until the desired temperature is reached. For juicier hamburgers, broil while still frozen. Meat to be breaded or deep-fried must be thawed first.

Don't bother to thaw cooked frozen stews before reheating. Keep covered while heating. Raw poultry should be thawed slowly before cooking except when making soup, in which case the chicken will thaw in the cooking liquid.

Some sauced dishes may need thickening after thawing. Add a little corn-starch or potato starch to a dab of sauce. Cook, then add to the dish.

Cheese Boeregs (Cheese Triangles)

These can be frozen before baking. Flash-freeze on baking sheets until solidly frozen. Stack between layers of foil in large box. Bake without thawing in 400°F oven for about 15 to 18 minutes.

Makes about 30 appetizers

1 pound phyllo pastry sheets
1 cup (2 sticks) unsalted butter or margarine, melted

1 pound Monterey Jack cheese, grated

1 egg, beaten
Salt

Unroll phyllo dough and place one sheet on work surface (keep remainder covered with waxed paper and damp towel to prevent drying). Brush phyllo with melted butter. Top with second sheet and brush with butter. Cut into lengthwise strips about 5 inches wide.

Combine cheese, egg and salt and mix well. Place about 1 tablespoon at one end of phyllo strip. Fold over to form triangle, then continue folding like a flag. Brush end with a little butter and carefully tuck into fold to seal. Repeat with remaining phyllo and filling.

Preheat oven to 400°F. Place triangles on ungreased baking sheet and brush again with butter. Bake until crisp and golden, 12 to 15 minutes. Serve warm.

Gorgonzola with Madeira

This hors d'oeuvre can be prepared and refrigerated two days ahead or frozen one week ahead, then unmolded before serving. Also excellent as a cheese course.

12 servings

½ pound (8 ounces) Gorgonzola cheese or bleu cheese, room temperature
½ cup (1 stick) unsalted butter, room temperature

1 tablespoon Madeira

Green grapes and sliced nectarines (garnish)

Cream first 3 ingredients in medium bowl until well blended. Pack cheese mixture into mold. Refrigerate until firm. (*Gorgonzola with Madeira can be prepared 2 days ahead to this point and refrigerated, or 1 week ahead and frozen.*)

To serve, invert mold onto platter and discard plastic wrap. Garnish with grapes and sliced nectarines.

Serve with crackers or French bread and apple slices.

Empanadas Chilenas (Chilean Turnovers)

Empanadas can be made ahead and frozen. The filling must be cold when the turnovers are prepared, so it's best to make it a day ahead.

Makes 24 empanadas

Filling
1 pound ground beef, crumbled
1 cup beef broth

3 tablespoons butter
4 large onions, chopped
2 tablespoons paprika
1½ teaspoons salt
1 teaspoon ground cumin
Ground red pepper to taste

Dough
1½ cups milk
1 cup (2 sticks) butter

5 cups all purpose flour
2 teaspoons baking powder
1 teaspoon salt
2 egg yolks, lightly beaten
3 hard-cooked eggs, sliced
1 2.3-ounce can sliced black olives, drained
1 egg beaten with 1 tablespoon water

For filling: Simmer meat in broth until it is no longer pink, 10 to 15 minutes. Meanwhile, melt 3 tablespoons butter in medium skillet over medium heat. Add onion and sauté until golden. Stir in paprika, salt, cumin and red pepper. Add to beef and simmer about 5 minutes. Taste and adjust seasoning if necessary. Let cool, then chill thoroughly.

For dough: Scald milk. Add butter and let melt over very low heat. Cool.

Combine flour, baking powder and salt in large bowl. Make well in center and add egg yolks. Stir in cooled milk and blend well. Turn out onto lightly floured surface and knead until smooth. Cover with towel and let rest in draft-free area about 20 minutes.

Preheat oven to 400°F. Lightly butter baking sheet. Divide dough into 4 pieces. Roll each into 10 × 15-inch rectangle. Using pastry wheel, cut each rectangle into six 5-inch squares. Place heaping tablespoon of filling on each square. Top with a few slices of egg and some of olives. Fold dough over filling (as for a letter). Moisten edges with a little water and press lightly to make them stick together. Fold over and seal ends in same way. Transfer to baking sheet. Repeat with remaining dough and filling. Brush with beaten egg and bake until golden, 35 to 40 minutes.

Sausage-Spinach Buns

These savory buns can be prepared ahead and frozen. For a crisp counterpoint, serve with romaine spears with a dip of sour cream, minced watercress and a touch of tarragon vinegar. Fresh cherries might provide a sweet ending. A glass or two of dry young white wine like a Vouvray or Chenin Blanc chilled in an icy stream would be welcome.

Makes 18 buns

Dough
- 1 envelope dry yeast
- 1½ cups warm water (105°F to 115°F)
- ½ cup olive oil
- 1½ teaspoons salt
- 2 to 2½ cups whole wheat flour
- 2 cups all purpose flour

Filling
- 1 pound hot Italian sausage
- ½ cup pine nuts
- 2 tablespoons olive oil
- 1 garlic clove, minced
- ½ pound fresh spinach (stems discarded), cooked and squeezed dry
- 1 cup ricotta cheese
- 1 egg, beaten
- Salt and freshly ground pepper
- 1 egg beaten with 1 teaspoon milk or cream

For dough: Dissolve yeast in water and let stand until foamy, about 10 minutes. Add olive oil, salt and enough of the flour so dough can be handled easily. Turn out onto generously floured surface and knead until dough is shiny and elastic. Place in greased bowl, turning to coat entire surface. Cover with towel and let rise until dough has doubled, about 1 hour.

For filling: Remove sausage from casings and crumble meat into skillet. Sauté over medium-high heat until no pink remains. Drain well and transfer to large mixing bowl. Wipe out skillet.

Using same skillet, cook pine nuts in olive oil until golden. Add garlic and cook briefly. Add to sausage along with spinach, ricotta and egg and mix well. Season to taste with salt and pepper.

Punch dough down and divide in half. Roll each half into 15 × 15-inch square. Cut into 5-inch squares. Place about 2 rounded tablespoons of filling on each square. Gather edges of dough around filling and press together to seal. Place buns pinched side down on ungreased baking sheet. Let stand in warm place for about 15 minutes.

Preheat oven to 425°F. Brush buns with egg mixture. Bake until golden, about 25 to 30 minutes. Let cool on wire racks. Serve at room temperature.

Onion Pancakes (Choan Yow Bang)

The pancakes can be rolled out in advance and frozen.

Makes five 4- to 5-inch pancakes

⅔ cup all purpose flour
¼ cup lukewarm water
　Lard or shortening
　Seasoned salt
5 tablespoons minced green onion
5 tablespoons crisp, crumbled bacon (about 4 strips)

3 tablespoons dehydrated onion flakes, moistened with water
　Sesame seed (optional)

2 teaspoons oil

Mix flour with water and knead 5 minutes. Divide into 5 portions and roll each into thin sheet (as thin as possible since the shape makes no difference at this point). Spread thin layer of lard or shortening over top. Sprinkle with seasoned salt and 1 tablespoon each green onion, bacon and onion flakes. Sprinkle with sesame seed if desired. Roll up jelly roll style. Coil into tight spiral and tuck ends under. Roll out into thin 4- or 5-inch round pancake.

Heat small skillet over medium-high heat. Add oil. Reduce heat and brown pancake on both sides until golden, about 1½ to 2 minutes per side. Repeat with remaining pancakes, adding more oil as necessary. Serve hot.

If preparing in advance, roll out pancakes but do not cook. Dust with flour and stack separately between sheets of waxed paper. Freeze. To serve, defrost overnight in refrigerator and follow above directions for preparation.

2 🍎 Soups

Few dishes are as uniquely satisfying as a bowl of soup, be it a robust, country-style combination of fresh vegetables and meat, or a smooth and elegant puree. Call it the ultimate comfort food: a pot of soup simmering away on the stove fills the kitchen with a wonderful aroma that few people fail to stop and savor.

Happily, soups are ideal make-ahead dishes. Main-course soups lend themselves admirably to advance preparation; in most cases their flavors actually benefit from a day or more of mingling. And lighter, first-course varieties are often only a matter of selecting and combining a few simple ingredients; refrigerating or freezing such soups is as uncomplicated as their initial preparation. Pureed vegetable soups freeze perfectly; but if cream is included in the recipe, it should be omitted before freezing, and stirred in only when the soup is reheated. Some soups, once made and stored, do not even need reheating: the Sour Cherry and Yogurt Soup on page 22, for example, is meant to be enjoyed chilled.

The most successful soups often take full advantage of the freshest and finest produce the markets have to offer. Often, the ingredients of a recipe can be varied depending on what is available and lowest in price; the Italian Country Vegetable Soup on page 20, for example, can change in character with the seasons. And, of course, its flavor only gets better if the soup is made a day or two in advance.

One make-ahead soup preparation that no kitchen should be without is stock based on meat, poultry or fish (see box, pages 18–19). Made in abundance, stock will keep in the freezer almost indefinitely, ready in an instant to thaw and become a flavorful addition to a sauce or braise, a delicious consommé, or the wholesome foundation for a soup that is quickly prepared yet tastes of hours of careful cooking.

Cream of Fresh Tomato Soup

Cream of Fresh Tomato Soup can be frozen. Garnish just before serving.

This fresh-tasting soup, textured with shreds of tomato and chives, is best served hot with a crusty loaf of bread.

4 servings

4 tablespoons vegetable oil (preferably cold-pressed safflower)
1 medium-size yellow onion, finely chopped
½ teaspoon finely chopped garlic
5 medium-size ripe tomatoes (unpeeled), sliced
2 tablespoons tomato paste
2 tablespoons whole wheat pastry flour
2 cups (or more) chicken stock or vegetable stock (or 2 cups water mixed with 2 teaspoons tamari soy sauce)

¾ cup half and half or double-strength reconstituted nonfat dry milk
Herb or vegetable salt
1 medium-size ripe tomato, peeled, seeded and cut julienne (garnish)
2 tablespoons finely chopped chives (garnish)

Heat 2 tablespoons oil in heavy 4-quart saucepan over low heat. Add onion and garlic and cook 1 minute. Add sliced tomato and continue cooking, stirring constantly, 5 minutes. Set aside. Combine tomato paste, flour and remaining oil in small bowl and mix well. Stir into tomato mixture. Add 2 cups stock and bring to boil over medium heat, stirring constantly. Remove from heat.

   Transfer mixture to processor or blender in batches and puree (or press through fine strainer). Return puree to saucepan. Place over low heat and cook 15 minutes. Add half and half. Stir in more stock if thinner consistency is desired. Season with herb salt to taste. Stir in tomato julienne and chives and warm through. Serve immediately.

Curried Green Pea and Tomato Soup

Curried Green Pea and Tomato Soup can be frozen. Garnish just before serving.

4 to 6 servings

¼ cup vegetable oil (preferably cold-pressed safflower)
1 medium-size yellow onion, finely chopped
1 teaspoon finely chopped garlic
4 cups fresh or thawed frozen green peas
¾ cup water
2 tablespoons whole wheat pastry flour
1 tablespoon curry powder
1 tablespoon tomato paste
½ teaspoon dry mustard
2 cups chicken stock or vegetable stock (or 2 cups water mixed with 2 teaspoons tamari soy sauce)

4 medium-size ripe tomatoes, peeled, seeded and sliced
1½ cups half and half or double-strength reconstituted nonfat dry milk
Herb or vegetable salt
½ cup finely shredded carrot (garnish)
1 tablespoon finely chopped fresh dill or 1½ teaspoons dried dillweed, crumbled (garnish)

Heat oil in heavy 4-quart saucepan over low heat. Add onion and garlic and cook until soft but not brown, about 3 minutes. Increase heat to medium, add peas and water and cook covered until peas are tender, about 5 minutes. Remove from heat and stir in flour, curry powder, tomato paste and mustard. Add stock and tomato and bring to boil over medium heat, stirring constantly.

Transfer mixture to processor or blender in batches and puree (or press through fine strainer). Stir in half and half and season with herb salt to taste. Let cool, cover and refrigerate.

Just before serving, blanch shredded carrot in rapidly boiling salted water. Drain well; pat dry with paper towels. Stir carrot into soup or use to garnish individual servings. Sprinkle with finely chopped fresh dill.

Tomato and Basil Soup

Tomato and Basil Soup can be frozen. Serve hot or chilled.

4 servings

4 tablespoons vegetable oil (preferably cold-pressed safflower)
1 medium-size yellow onion, chopped
½ teaspoon finely chopped garlic
2 pounds ripe tomatoes (unpeeled), sliced
1 cup lightly packed fresh basil leaves
1 tablespoon tomato paste
1 teaspoon honey
1 bay leaf

2 teaspoons cornstarch or potato flour
3 cups chicken stock or vegetable stock (or 3 cups water mixed with 3 teaspoons tamari soy sauce)
Herb or vegetable salt
Freshly ground pepper
1 medium-size ripe tomato, peeled, seeded and cut julienne (garnish)
2 tablespoons finely chopped fresh basil or parsley (optional)

Heat 3 tablespoons oil in heavy 4-quart saucepan over medium heat. Add onion and garlic and cook until onion is soft but not brown, about 5 minutes. Add sliced tomato and continue cooking 3 minutes. Stir in basil, tomato paste, honey and bay leaf. Reduce heat to low, cover and cook 10 minutes.

Transfer mixture to processor or blender in batches and puree. Press through fine strainer to remove remaining tomato skin and seeds. Return puree to saucepan. Combine cornstarch and remaining oil in small bowl. Stir into puree. Add stock and bring to boil over medium heat, stirring constantly. Reduce heat to low and simmer 10 minutes. Season with herb salt and pepper to taste. Stir in tomato julienne and chopped basil and serve.

Potage Puree Crecy

Potage can be frozen. Defrost in refrigerator overnight before reheating over low heat.

6 to 8 servings

¼ cup (½ stick) butter
1½ pounds carrots, thinly sliced
1 large onion (about ½ pound), thinly sliced
¾ pound baking potatoes, unpeeled and thinly sliced
1½ cups chicken stock
Pinch of sugar

1½ cups milk, scalded
1 cup half and half
2 egg yolks, beaten
Salt and freshly ground white pepper
Minced fresh chives and parsley (garnish)
Fried croutons (garnish)

Melt butter in heavy 3-quart saucepan over medium heat. Add carrot, onion and potatoes and sauté until onion is golden brown. Stir in stock and sugar, reduce heat and simmer until vegetables are very soft (test by mashing with back of spoon). Transfer to food processor or blender in batches and puree.

Return to saucepan and place over low heat. Gradually stir in milk, blending well. Combine half and half with yolks and blend into puree. Bring to simmer, stirring frequently. Season to taste with salt and pepper. Serve hot, garnished with chives, parsley, croutons.

Celery and Almond Soup

This soup is best when made ahead and refrigerated for a day or two.

2 servings

2 tablespoons (¼ stick) butter
½ pound celery (about 3 large stalks), chopped
¼ teaspoon curry powder or to taste
1 cup chicken broth
2 teaspoons minced fresh parsley

1 cup milk
Salt and freshly ground pepper

2 tablespoons whipping cream
2 tablespoons slivered almonds, toasted

Melt butter in medium saucepan over low heat. Add celery and curry and cook about 10 minutes, stirring occasionally. Stir in broth and parsley and bring to boil over high heat. Reduce heat to low, cover and simmer 20 minutes. Blend in milk, salt and pepper.

Transfer to blender and mix until almost smooth (there will be tiny crunchy bits of celery that give the soup a pleasing texture). Return to low heat and warm through. Stir in cream and almonds just before serving.

Spanish Garlic and Avocado Soup

Soup can be prepared several days ahead.

Don't be put off by the six cloves of garlic. After simmering in stock, they become rich and mellow.

6 to 8 servings

2 tablespoons (¼ stick) unsalted butter
1 medium onion, chopped
4 cups rich chicken stock
6 large garlic cloves

1 large ripe avocado, peeled, seeded and chopped

Juice of ½ lime
1½ cups buttermilk
Salt and freshly ground pepper
Minced green onion tops or freshly snipped chives (garnish)

Melt butter in 3-quart saucepan over medium heat. Add onion and sauté until soft. Add stock and garlic and bring to simmer. Cover and cook 30 minutes. Let mixture cool slightly.

Puree in batches in processor or blender. Transfer to large serving bowl. Puree avocado and lime juice and add to stock. Blend in buttermilk and season with salt and pepper to taste. Serve hot or cold garnished with minced green onion tops or fresh chives.

Velouté of Fennel

Stock mixture can be prepared in advance. Thicken and season just before serving.

8 servings

4 tablespoons (½ stick) unsalted butter
6 large heads fennel, trimmed and thinly sliced
6 tablespoons (¾ stick) unsalted butter
6 tablespoons all purpose flour

8 cups chicken stock, preferably homemade

4 egg yolks
¾ cup whipping cream
Salt and freshly ground pepper
Chopped fresh chives (garnish)

Melt 4 tablespoons butter in large skillet over medium heat. Add fennel, cover and slowly braise until completely softened and lightly browned, stirring occasionally, about 30 minutes. Transfer to processor and puree.

Melt remaining butter in large heavy saucepan over medium-low heat. Add flour and stir with wooden spoon until flour is cooked but still light in color, about 15 minutes. Slowly add stock to flour mixture, beating constantly. Bring to boil. Reduce heat to low and simmer gently 30 minutes. Stir in fennel. Pass soup through fine strainer, if desired. *(Can be prepared ahead.)*

Just before serving, bring soup to simmer. Combine egg yolks and cream in small bowl and beat well. *Gradually* add about 1 cup stock to yolk mixture, beating constantly. Slowly blend yolk mixture back into remaining stock. (Be careful not to let soup boil or eggs will curdle.) Season to taste with salt and pepper. Garnish with chives.

If fresh fennel is unavailable, substitute 1 pound celery and 1 tablespoon fennel seed.

Lemon Egg Soup with Fresh Chives

Soup base can be prepared several days ahead. Reheat before thickening, garnish and serve.

8 servings

6 cups chicken stock
1 pound chicken wings, backs and giblets, cut up
1 medium carrot, chopped
1 medium celery stalk (including leaves), coarsely chopped

½ cup long-grain rice

Salt and freshly ground pepper

4 eggs
¼ cup fresh lemon juice
Lemon slices (garnish)
¼ cup snipped fresh chives (garnish)

Combine first four ingredients in 4-quart saucepan over medium heat. Simmer for 40 to 45 minutes. Let cool. Skim off fat. Strain stock into bowl, pressing vegetables (with wooden spoon) to add texture and flavor.

Return stock to saucepan and bring to boil. Add rice, reduce heat and cook over medium heat until rice is tender, about 20 minutes. Add salt and pepper to taste. *(Soup can be made several days ahead to this point and refrigerated. Reheat slowly before adding to eggs.)*

Just before serving, beat eggs in medium bowl until smooth. Add ¼ cup hot stock to eggs, then whisk back into remaining stock. Stir in lemon juice and heat through. Ladle soup into bowls or tureen. Garnish with lemon and chives.

🍎 Basic Stocks for Storage

A good meat or fish stock is a valuable make-ahead asset. Easily prepared in large quantities, it can be frozen in smaller portions and stored indefinitely (milk cartons make ideal containers). Use it as a base for hearty soups, or as a poaching or braising liquid. Or serve it on its own as a delicate consommé.

Meat Stock

Makes 3 to 4 quarts

Meats
- 2 pounds of beef soup bones
- 2 pounds chicken bones, giblets and backs
- 3 pounds beef (stew meat, short ribs or chuck)
- 1 3-pound fryer chicken, cut in half lengthwise

Vegetables
- 3 stalks celery with leaves
- 3 carrots, unpeeled, scrubbed
- 3 leeks, cleaned and split (reserve green tops)
- 1 large onion, unpeeled, root end removed
- 2 parsnips or turnips
- 6 parsley sprigs
- 5 garlic cloves, unpeeled, lightly crushed

Seasonings
- 3 sprigs fresh dill or 2 teaspoons dried
- 1 teaspoon thyme
- 2 bay leaves
- 6 whole cloves
- 1 teaspoon whole allspice
- 3 ⅛-inch slices fresh ginger or 1 teaspoon ground
- 1 teaspoon peppercorns
- 2 teaspoons salt

Arrange beef and chicken bones in bottom of 12- to 16-quart stockpot. Add beef, celery, carrots, leeks (white part only), onion, parsnips or turnips, parsley, garlic and seasonings. Add enough cold water to cover ¾ of contents. Slowly bring to a simmer and cook uncovered 1 hour.

Add chicken halves and cover soup with green leek tops to keep flavors from evaporating. Simmer 1 hour longer or until soup has a rich flavor.

Let vegetables and meat cool in broth. When cool, remove meat and bones. Reserve meat. With a wooden spoon press vegetables through strainer, returning juices to soup. Strain broth into 6-quart bowl or pan. Return meat to broth. Refrigerate overnight.

Minestrone Cortonese

This soup can be prepared up to four days ahead and refrigerated.

A hearty main-dish vegetable soup from the village of Cortona in Tuscany.

6 servings

- 1 cup dried navy (pea) beans
- 4 cups peeled and cubed potato
- 2 cups chopped yellow onion
- 2 cups dry white wine or water
- 1 cup very thinly sliced carrot
- 2 teaspoons finely chopped garlic
- ⅓ cup virgin olive oil (preferably cold-pressed)
- 2 teaspoons herb or vegetable salt
- 1 teaspoon sea salt or 2 teaspoons coarse salt
- 4 cups finely shredded fresh spinach (about 1 bunch)
- 1½ cups freshly grated Parmesan cheese

Discard any discolored beans. Rinse remainder under cold running water. Drain well. Transfer to large bowl. Add enough cold water to allow beans to expand at

Discard solid layer of fat on top of chilled soup. Reheat stock and season to taste with salt and pepper.

Basic White Wine Fish Stock

Before using for a sauce or soup, boil fish stock and reduce to intensify flavor. Add salt only after reducing stock and combining it with other ingredients.

Makes about 1 quart

3 pounds fish bones (heads, frames, trimmings), rinsed, dried and cut into 3-inch pieces
2 tablespoons (¼ stick) butter
1 leek (white part only), sliced
1 small carrot, sliced
1 small celery stalk (with leaves), sliced
2 ounces mushroom stems (optional)

10 parsley sprigs (with stems)
6 fresh thyme sprigs or 2 teaspoons dried thyme, crumbled
½ bay leaf
6 white peppercorns, coarsely crushed
3 1½-inch strips lemon peel
2 cups dry white wine
5 cups (about) cold water

Discard any feathery red gills from fish heads if necessary (this will prevent stock from tasting bitter). Melt butter in heavy nonaluminum 8-quart pot over low heat. Add fish and next 7 ingredients. Cover and cook, stirring occasionally, until vegetables are translucent, about 10 minutes. Add peppercorns and lemon peel and blend well. Pour in wine and enough water just to cover ingredients (liquids should not be warm, or juices will be sealed in rather than extracted). Bring mixture slowly to simmering point. Partially cover pan and reduce heat until liquid is just shaking (do not boil, or stock will be cloudy). Cook, skimming foam from surface as necessary, until stock is richly flavored, about 35 minutes.

Line fine sieve or strainer with several layers of dampened cheesecloth and set over large bowl. Strain stock into bowl, pressing down lightly on fish and vegetables with back of spoon to extract as much liquid as possible. Let cool. Refrigerate. Discard fat that accumulates on surface. Store stock in refrigerator, or freeze. If refrigerating, reboil every 3 days to prevent spoilage.
Recipe can be halved or doubled.

least 2½ times, about 2½ to 3 cups. Let soak at least 8 hours or overnight. (Beans can be quick-soaked. Boil 2 to 3 minutes. Remove from heat, cover and let soak for 1 hour.)

Transfer beans and soaking liquid to heavy large saucepan or Dutch oven. Add water as necessary so liquid covers beans by 1 inch. Bring to boil over medium-high heat. Cover tightly, reduce heat to low and cook until beans are tender, about 1 hour. Stir in potato, onion, wine, carrot, garlic, olive oil and salts. If necessary, add more water so ingredients are covered by 1 inch of liquid. Increase heat to high and bring soup to boil. Cover, reduce heat to low and simmer until vegetables are tender but not mushy, about 30 minutes. Season to taste.

Stir in spinach and ½ cup cheese. Remove soup from heat and let stand briefly until spinach is wilted. Ladle soup into large bowls. Pass remaining Parmesan cheese separately.

Kidney Bean and Lentil Soup with Sorrel

Bean and Lentil Soup can be prepared ahead and frozen. Before serving, reheat soup and combine with sorrel mixture.

8 servings

1 cup dried kidney beans
1 cup lentils
2 medium-size yellow onions, chopped
1 large celery stalk, chopped
1 carrot, chopped
4 parsley sprigs
1 teaspoon chopped garlic
1 bay leaf
1 teaspoon sea salt or 2 teaspoons coarse salt
3 cups good quality chicken stock (or 3 cups water combined with 1½ tablespoons tamari sauce)

2 tablespoons vegetable oil (preferably cold-pressed safflower)
4 cups shredded sorrel (or 4 cups shredded fresh spinach tossed with 1 to 2 tablespoons fresh lemon juice)
½ cup chopped fresh parsley
  Plain yogurt (garnish)
  Ground red pepper (garnish)

Discard any discolored kidney beans. Rinse remainder under cold running water. Drain well. Transfer to large bowl. Add enough cold water to allow beans to expand at least 2½ times, about 2½ to 3 cups. Let soak at least 8 hours or overnight. (Beans can be quick-soaked. Boil 2 to 3 minutes. Remove from heat, cover and let stand at room temperature for 1 hour.)

Transfer beans and soaking liquid to heavy large saucepan or Dutch oven. Add lentils, onion, celery, carrot, parsley, garlic, bay leaf, salt and stock and bring to boil over medium-high heat. Cover, reduce heat to low and simmer until beans are tender, about 1 hour. Puree mixture in processor or blender. Adjust seasoning. *(Soup can be prepared ahead to this point and frozen.)*

Heat oil in large skillet over low heat. Add sorrel and chopped parsley and stir until sorrel wilts and loses color. Return soup to saucepan and blend in sorrel mixture. Heat through over medium-low heat. Ladle into bowls. Garnish with yogurt and sprinkle lightly with ground red pepper.

Italian Country Vegetable Soup

Soup is best if prepared one or two days ahead. Any leftovers can be frozen.

Fill your soup pot with all the in-season vegetables available and accent their flavors with the herb-based Pesto Sauce. Try this thick soup hot during the winter, but serve it cold when the warm winds blow. For a complete meal, add hot Italian bread, fruit and cheese.

10 to 12 servings

1½ cups dried Great Northern or cannellini beans, soaked overnight in cold water
  Salted water

1½ to 2 pounds Savoy cabbage
½ pound spinach
1 teaspoon salt

3 tablespoons olive oil
3 ounces prosciutto, chopped
½ cup chopped fresh parsley (Italian preferred)
2 garlic cloves, minced
¼ pound green beans, cut into 1-inch pieces

¼ pound zucchini, sliced
2 celery stalks, diced
1 large carrot, sliced about ¼-inch thick
1 medium potato, thinly sliced
1 medium red onion, thinly sliced
1 to 1½ quarts degreased chicken or beef broth
1 tablespoon tomato paste

2 cups degreased beef or chicken broth
½ cup uncooked long-grain rice
  Pesto Sauce (see following recipe)
  Freshly grated Parmesan cheese

Drain beans well. Transfer to medium saucepan and cover with salted water. Bring to boil, reduce heat to medium-low and simmer about 20 to 25 minutes (beans will be only partially cooked). Drain and set aside.

Thoroughly wash and then shred cabbage and spinach. Combine in 6- to 8-quart Dutch oven with water that clings to leaves. Sprinkle with salt. Cook over low heat until greens are wilted, about 15 minutes. Transfer to colander and drain well. Squeeze dry and set aside.

Heat oil in Dutch oven over medium-high heat. Add prosciutto, parsley and garlic and sauté until lightly browned. Add remaining vegetables and sauté an additional 5 minutes, stirring frequently. Mix in reserved beans, cabbage and spinach and blend well. Pour in enough broth to cover. Stir in tomato paste. Bring mixture to boil, reduce heat and simmer gently, uncovered, until all ingredients are tender, about 40 minutes, stirring often.

If serving soup hot: Bring 2 cups broth to boil in 2-quart saucepan over medium-high heat. Add rice, reduce heat to medium and continue cooking until rice is almost tender. Drain, reserving broth, and add rice to soup. If soup then appears too thick, stir in a portion of rice cooking liquid. Serve in individual bowls topped with a spoonful of Pesto Sauce and a sprinkling of Parmesan cheese.

If serving soup cold: Follow above directions except cover and chill thoroughly. Omit pesto and serve only with a sprinkling of Parmesan.

Pesto Sauce

½ cup fresh basil leaves (about 15 with stems removed) or 2 teaspoons dried	½ cup freshly grated Parmesan or Pecorino cheese
½ cup parsley leaves (Italian preferred)	⅓ cup pine nuts or walnuts
	2 to 4 garlic cloves, minced
	¼ to ½ cup imported olive oil

Place first 5 ingredients in blender or food processor and puree, adding olive oil a little at a time until mixture forms soft paste.

Old-Fashioned Vegetable Beef Soup

Soup can be prepared ahead and refrigerated. Reheat and garnish with parsley before serving.

6 to 8 servings

Stock
1 8-pound whole beef brisket, trimmed, flat cut portion removed and reserved for roasting
2 pounds (about) oxtail bones, cut to thickness of 6 to 8 inches
4 to 5 pounds (about) beef marrow bones, cut to thickness of 8 to 10¾ inches
3 medium leeks, halved and thoroughly rinsed
5 medium turnips, peeled and halved
6 parsley sprigs
4 celery stalks (with leaves), halved crosswise
6 medium carrots
6 pounds fresh tomatoes, halved, or 2 28-ounce cans peeled tomatoes, undrained
1 16-ounce can tomato juice

8 cups (2 quarts) beef consommé (preferably homemade)
8 cups (2 quarts) water
6 peppercorns
½ teaspoon salt

Vegetables
2 celery hearts, sliced
6 medium carrots
1 10-ounce package frozen limas, thawed
1 pound petits pois or 1 16-ounce package frozen tiny peas, thawed

1½ cups barley, cooked 1½ hours and drained
½ cup coarsely chopped fresh parsley (garnish)

For stock: Combine all ingredients in large stockpot over medium-high heat and bring to boil. Reduce heat, cover and simmer until beef brisket is tender, approximately 4 to 5 hours.

Remove stock from heat. Transfer bones to work surface using slotted spoon. Trim meat from bones and set aside, discarding fat and bones. Trim off any remaining fat from brisket. Cut all meat into small pieces; add to stockpot.

Strain stock through medium sieve set over large mixing bowl, pressing vegetables with back of wooden spoon to extract as much liquid as possible. Return stock to pot (make sure meat is completely covered with liquid). Cover and refrigerate overnight.

Bring small amount of water to boil in steamer. Add celery hearts and steam until crisp-tender, about 3½ minutes. Repeat for carrots, steaming 3½ minutes, lima beans, steaming 2 minutes, and peas, steaming 2 to 3 minutes.

Skim fat from surface of stock (or blot with paper towel) and discard. Stir in barley and vegetables. *(Soup can be prepared ahead to this point, covered and refrigerated.)* Place over medium heat and bring to gentle boil, stirring occasionally. Transfer soup to tureen. Sprinkle individual servings with parsley.

Cabbage Borscht

For the best flavor, prepare at least a day ahead. Borscht can be prepared up to three days ahead or stored in freezer if desired.

The succulent blending of sweet and sour flavors highlights this hearty meal-in-one soup. Serve topped with sour cream and accompanied by hot crusty rye bread studded with caraway seeds.

10 to 12 servings

4 pounds lean meaty short ribs (flanken)
2½ quarts (10 cups) beef stock
1 16-ounce can whole tomatoes, undrained
2 large onions, minced
3 to 4 marrow bones
3 garlic cloves, minced
5 pounds green cabbage, cored, coarsely shredded

½ pound sauerkraut, undrained
¼ to ½ cup fresh lemon juice
¼ to ½ cup sugar
Salt and freshly ground pepper
2 tablespoons cornstarch dissolved in ½ cup dry red wine
Sour cream (garnish)

Combine first 6 ingredients in 8-quart stockpot and bring to boil, skimming off any foam that accumulates on surface. Add cabbage and sauerkraut, reduce heat, cover and simmer until meat is tender, about 2 hours. Blend in lemon juice and sugar to taste (soup should have sweet-sour flavor). Season with salt and pepper. Blend in cornstarch mixture, stirring until slightly thickened. Degrease. Serve hot topped with a dollop of sour cream.

Sour Cherry and Yogurt Soup

The soup should be prepared a day in advance. It works well as a first course, dessert or snack. For a tart soup, ¼ cup sugar is perfect.

4 servings

2 cups plain yogurt (homemade or commercial)
Pinch of salt
½ pound pitted fresh or thawed frozen sour cherries, undrained *(do not use canned)*

½ teaspoon grated orange zest
Honey or sugar to taste

Combine yogurt and salt in food processor or blender and mix until smooth and liquid. Add cherries and juice and blend briefly (there should be small pieces of fruit remaining). Pour into bowl and stir in zest and honey or sugar. Chill at least 24 hours before serving.

Duck and Roasted Onion Potage

This rich soup can be pre-pared ahead and frozen up to two months. Reheat and serve with Classic French Bread (see recipe, page 82) and a watercress salad. A medium-full red Bordeaux or Côtes du Rhône or a California Cabernet Sauvignon is the perfect complement.

6 servings

5 medium onions, unpeeled
1 4- to 5-pound duck, quartered and patted dry (reserve duck liver)
3 tablespoons Madeira

1 large onion, chopped
2 medium turnips, chopped
20 large garlic cloves, peeled
½ cup dry white wine
5 to 6 tablespoons Verdelho or Sercial Madeira, or to taste
9 cups rich chicken stock

3 cups chopped peeled new potatoes (about 2 large)
1½ cups chopped peeled turnip (about 2 medium)
½ cup chopped carrot (about 1 small)

1 cup light cream
Salt and freshly ground pepper

3 tablespoons minced fresh parsley (garnish)

Preheat oven to 425°F. Place sheet of aluminum foil over oven rack. Arrange 5 medium onions on foil. Roast until easily pierced with fork, about 1¼ hours. Let cool. *(Onions can be prepared 3 days ahead and refrigerated.)*

Place duck liver in small container. Add 3 tablespoons Madeira. Cover and marinate in refrigerator.

Preheat broiler. Arrange duck on broiler rack. Prick skin thoroughly. Brown duck well on both sides, about 15 minutes. Remove from oven. Remove skin from duck and reserve.

Transfer 3 tablespoons duck fat from broiler pan to heavy 6-quart stockpot over high heat. Add 1 chopped onion and 2 chopped turnips and cook, stirring frequently, until well browned. Add garlic and skinned duck and cook 1 minute. Pour in wine and Madeira and bring to boil, scraping up any browned bits. Boil 2 to 3 minutes. Reduce heat and add stock. Cover partially and simmer 1½ hours. Transfer duck pieces to platter and let cool. *(Soup can be prepared ahead to this point and refrigerated overnight.)*

Skim all fat from soup. Peel roasted onions and add to soup with potatoes, 1½ cups turnip and ½ cup carrot. Simmer over low heat until vegetables are tender, about 30 minutes.

Meanwhile, shred duck meat, discarding bones. Cut skin into thin julienne.

Cook skin in medium skillet over medium heat until crisp and golden. Drain on paper towels. Drain liquid from duck liver into soup. Cut liver into thin julienne and set aside.

Transfer soup to processor or blender in batches and puree. *(Soup can be prepared ahead to this point and frozen up to 2 months.)* Return to stockpot and reheat. Stir in cream, salt and pepper.

Add reserved duck meat, crisp skin and liver to stockpot. Cook until heated through, about 3 minutes. Sprinkle with fresh parsley and serve.

Cold Sorrel Soup

Soup can be made up to two days ahead.

Use spinach if sorrel is not available, adding 1 teaspoon of lemon juice to the skillet while sautéing.

6 to 8 servings

1 pound fresh sorrel or spinach

2 tablespoons (¼ stick) unsalted butter

1 teaspoon fresh lemon juice (if using spinach)

4 cups chicken stock

1 cup whipping cream

6 egg yolks

1 teaspoon chopped chervil
Salt and freshly ground white pepper

Wash sorrel thoroughly in cold water; discard stems and any bruised leaves. Stack leaves and roll up lengthwise. Cut crosswise as thinly as possible.

Melt butter in skillet over medium heat. Add sorrel (or spinach and lemon juice) and cook until very limp, stirring constantly. Remove from heat.

Bring stock to simmer in 3-quart saucepan. Whisk cream with yolks. Pour small amount of hot stock into cream mixture and blend well. Slowly add to simmering stock in thin stream, whisking constantly. Reduce heat to low and continue cooking, whisking constantly, until soup has thickened and coats back of metal spoon, about 5 minutes *(do not allow to boil, or soup will curdle)*.

Strain into bowl. Blend in sorrel, chervil, salt and pepper. Cool to room temperature, then chill before serving.

3 ❦ Salads

Think of salads and you instantly think of freshness: a cool mixture of crisp leaves, tossed with its dressing just prior to serving. Such a creation is so simple that you might not imagine making it in advance. Yet, if you like, you can do just that. The vinaigrette may be mixed in the bottom of a large salad bowl an hour or so before the meal. To keep the greens from soaking in the dressing and wilting, the salad servers are crossed over the vinaigrette and a few large whole leaves are placed on top of the servers. Then the remaining torn leaves and other ingredients are piled into the bowl and the salad is kept cool until ready for tossing.

Beyond the classic bowl of tossed greens, of course, salads come in endless variety, and many of them—including those featured on the pages that follow—hold up well or even benefit from advance preparation. Some, such as Zucchini in Watercress Dressing (page 26), are meant to be served thoroughly chilled, and require at least several hours of refrigeration. Others, such as Early Dutch Coleslaw (page 26), need a few hours for their texture to soften and flavors to mingle. Salads of roasted peppers (page 27) or artichokes and mushrooms (page 28) are often marinated, soaking for several days in well-seasoned dressings. Still other salads can be partly prepared in advance: potatoes boiled and mixed with their dressing for a platter of Papaya and Potato Salad with avocado and ham (page 31); lemon containers hollowed and frozen, radishes and carrots peeled and shredded, for the Japanese salad Kohaku Namasu (page 27).

Any salad, whether prepared minutes before serving or days ahead of time, will benefit from some simple advance planning. By employing the tips on page 28, you will find yourself not only saving time in the kitchen but also, in the bargain, becoming even more creative.

Zucchini in Watercress Dressing

This salad can be assembled a day or two in advance.

2 servings

3 tablespoons olive oil
1½ teaspoons fresh lemon juice
1 teaspoon white wine vinegar
½ teaspoon Dijon mustard
Pinch of dried tarragon

Salt and freshly ground pepper
2 zucchini, halved lengthwise and thinly sliced
¼ cup watercress leaves, minced

Whisk oil, lemon juice, vinegar, mustard, tarragon, salt and pepper in small bowl. Add zucchini and watercress and toss gently. Cover and chill until serving time.

Marinated Coleslaw

Can be refrigerated two weeks.

12 servings

1 cup oil
¾ cup sugar
¾ cup cider vinegar
1 large head cabbage (about 3 pounds), shredded
2 medium carrots, coarsely grated

1 medium onion, shredded
1 green bell pepper, seeded and coarsely chopped
1 tablespoon dry mustard, sifted
1 heaping teaspoon celery seed
½ teaspoon salt

Combine oil, sugar and vinegar in medium saucepan and bring to boil over medium-high heat.

Meanwhile, combine cabbage, carrot, onion and pepper in large bowl. Sprinkle with mustard, celery seed and salt and toss to blend well. Pour hot oil mixture over vegetables and mix well. Chill 24 hours. Drain salad well before serving.

Early Dutch Coleslaw

Can be prepared three days ahead. Surround with cabbage leaves for attractive serving.

The dressing for this delicious coleslaw dates back to the first Dutch settlers in America.

12 servings

Dressing
3 eggs
¾ cup cider vinegar
1½ tablespoons dry mustard
2 teaspoons sugar (optional)
1 teaspoon salt
½ teaspoon celery seed
⅛ teaspoon freshly ground pepper

3 tablespoons butter or bacon fat
2 tablespoons all purpose flour
1 cup milk

Coleslaw
7 cups shredded green cabbage
¾ cup minced onion
½ cup chopped pimiento
½ cup sour cream
¼ cup minced celery
¼ cup minced green pepper
3 tablespoons minced fresh parsley
Salt and freshly ground pepper

For dressing: Combine eggs, vinegar, mustard, sugar, salt, celery seed and pepper in medium mixing bowl and beat until smooth. Set aside.

Melt butter in heavy nonaluminum 1½-quart saucepan over medium heat. Stir in flour and cook, whisking constantly, about 3 minutes, reducing heat if necessary so flour does not brown. Pour in milk and continue whisking until sauce begins to simmer. Cook, whisking constantly, about 5 minutes. Reduce heat to just below simmer, stir in egg mixture and cook until sauce thickens; do not boil, or eggs will curdle. Remove from heat and let cool. Season to taste. Transfer to container, cover and refrigerate up to 5 days.

For coleslaw: Combine cabbage, onion, pimiento, sour cream, celery, pepper and parsley in large mixing bowl and toss lightly. Add dressing and toss again. Season with salt and pepper to taste. Cover and refrigerate 1 to 3 days.

Kohaku Namasu (Radish and Carrot Salad in Lemon Cups)

The vegetables can be prepared five days ahead and refrigerated. Lemon shells can be frozen until day they are served.

Use as a first-course salad or garnish.

Makes 12 salad cups

6 small lemons
   Rice vinegar
¼ cup sugar
¼ teaspoon salt

1½ cups julienne of peeled daikon (Japanese white radish)
    Salt
¼ cup julienne of peeled carrot

Cut lemons in half. Squeeze juice into measuring cup. Scoop out pulp and discard, reserving lemon shells. Trim bottoms so halves stand upright. If using within 2 hours, stuff each with damp paper towels. (Cover shells with plastic and freeze if preparing ahead.)

Add enough vinegar to lemon juice to equal ½ cup. Transfer to small saucepan. Add sugar and ¼ teaspoon salt and cook over low heat just until sugar and salt dissolve. Remove sauce from heat, cover and refrigerate.

Place radish julienne in medium bowl. Sprinkle lightly with salt. Let stand 2 to 3 minutes. Squeeze to wilt slightly; drain well. (If radish is strongly flavored, soak in cold water 5 minutes and squeeze dry.) Repeat for carrot.

Combine carrot and radish in large bowl. Pour chilled lemon sauce over vegetables. *(Can be made 5 days ahead to this point, covered and refrigerated.)* Let stand at room temperature at least 30 minutes. To serve, drain vegetables well. Mound into lemon shells. Serve chilled or at room temperature.

Roasted Pepper Salad

Salad can be prepared ahead and refrigerated up to one week.

12 servings

3 green bell peppers
2 red bell peppers

1 6-ounce jar marinated artichoke hearts, drained (marinade reserved) and patted dry
   Olive oil
½ pound feta cheese, rinsed, patted dry and crumbled
2 6-ounce cans black olives, drained

¾ cup fresh mushrooms, sliced
8 tablespoons sliced green onion
6 tablespoons minced fresh parsley
2 teaspoons minced garlic
1½ tablespoons dried oregano, crumbled
   Juice of 1½ lemons
   Salt and freshly ground pepper

   Toasted sesame seed or additional feta cheese (garnish)

Preheat oven to 450°F. Place peppers on baking sheet and roast until skins are black and peppers are soft, about 30 minutes. Let cool slightly. Peel off skin. Cut peppers in half and discard stem and seeds; slice peppers thinly. Transfer to large serving bowl (preferably glass).

Combine reserved artichoke marinade in measuring cup with enough olive oil to equal 1⅓ cups. Pour over peppers. Add all remaining ingredients except garnish and toss well. Refrigerate at least 24 hours. *(Can be prepared up to 1 week ahead to this point and refrigerated.)*

To serve, garnish with sesame seed or feta cheese. Serve at room temperature.

🍎 *Timesaving Salad Tips*

- Use only the freshest and best produce of the season. Check carefully for bruises, soft spots and discoloration when selecting.
- Each individual salad ingredient can be peeled, chopped, torn, sliced or otherwise prepared in advance and refrigerated until ready to use.
- If meat, seafood or poultry is to be added, cook it the day before, allow to cool, wrap tightly and refrigerate overnight.
- Recipes for most dressings can easily be doubled or tripled and the remainder reserved for other salads later in the week.
- If you have a home vegetable garden, take advantage of a bountiful crop to add new dimensions to basic tossed salads.
- Use leftovers from one salad as the basis for another.

Marinated Artichokes and Mushrooms

Can be prepared ahead of time. Strain before serving.

4 to 6 servings

1 cup water
½ cup cider vinegar
1 9-ounce package frozen artichoke halves
½ pound fresh medium to large mushrooms, trimmed

⅓ cup virgin olive oil
¼ cup cider vinegar
Juice of 1 medium lemon
1 tablespoon chopped green onion (green part only)

1 teaspoon tamari soy sauce
1 medium garlic clove, crushed
1 teaspoon dried oregano, crumbled
½ teaspoon dried marjoram, crumbled
½ teaspoon dried thyme, crumbled
½ teaspoon dried basil, crumbled
Freshly ground pepper

Combine water and vinegar in 3-quart stainless steel saucepan and bring to boil over high heat. Add artichoke halves and immediately remove from heat. Let stand 4 to 5 minutes. Remove artichokes and pan using slotted spoon and let cool. Add mushrooms to same liquid. Place over high heat and bring to boil. Let boil until mushrooms are just tender, about 5 to 8 minutes. Drain well; let cool.

Transfer artichokes and mushrooms to 1-quart glass jar with tight-fitting lid. Add oil, vinegar, lemon juice, green onion, soy sauce, garlic, herbs and pepper and shake well. Refrigerate at least 24 hours, shaking jar occasionally. Strain and discard liquid before using.

Mushroom, Fennel and Pepperoni Salad

Preparations can be started one day ahead. Salad is tossed with pepperoni and parsley just before serving.

6 servings

1 pound large fresh mushrooms, sliced
1 cup fennel or celery, cut julienne
1 red bell pepper, roasted, peeled and diced, or 1 pimiento, diced
1 cup olive oil
2 tablespoons minced hot chili pepper
1 tablespoon minced garlic
½ cup red wine vinegar

2 teaspoons fennel seed
1½ teaspoons salt
¼ teaspoon freshly ground pepper
2 bay leaves, crushed

¾ cup thinly sliced pepperoni
¼ cup chopped fresh parsley
6 lettuce leaves
 Ripe Greek or Niçoise olives (garnish)

Combine mushrooms, fennel and red pepper in large bowl. Combine oil, hot chili pepper and garlic in 1-quart saucepan and simmer over medium-high heat until garlic is golden, about 10 minutes. Stir in vinegar, fennel seed, salt, pepper and bay leaves and simmer an additional 3 minutes. Remove from heat and cool slightly. Pour over mushrooms and toss well. Cover and refrigerate 4 to 24 hours.

Just before serving, add pepperoni and parsley and toss again. Center lettuce leaf on each salad plate and top evenly with mushroom mixture. Garnish with Greek or Niçoise olives.

Vegetable Rice Salad

Perfect with cold roasted meat and chicken, this salad can be made one day ahead and chilled. Bring to room temperature before serving.

6 servings

Vegetable Rice Salad
2 cups cooked long-grain brown rice
¼ cup finely sliced radishes (about 3 large)
½ cup peeled, seeded and finely diced cucumbers
½ cup finely diced red bell pepper
¼ cup finely diced celery
¼ cup thinly sliced green onion
 Salt and freshly ground white pepper

Dressing
¼ cup olive oil
¼ cup freshly grated Parmesan cheese

3 tablespoons cider vinegar
2 tablespoons plain yogurt
1 tablespoon minced fresh basil (or other fresh herb)
½ teaspoon prepared mustard
½ teaspoon salt
¼ teaspoon freshly ground pepper

 Lettuce leaves (garnish)
 Tomato wedges (garnish)
2 tablespoons toasted pumpkin seed (optional garnish)

For salad: Combine all ingredients in large bowl. Taste and adjust seasoning.
For dressing: Blend all ingredients in medium mixing bowl.
Add dressing to salad, mixing well. Taste and adjust seasoning. Cover tightly and refrigerate overnight.
Bring salad to room temperature. Arrange lettuce leaves on large serving platter. Toss salad lightly and mound in center. Garnish with tomato wedges. Sprinkle with toasted pumpkin seed.

Tart Rice Salad

This unusual salad can be prepared up to three days ahead.

2 servings

1 cup water
Generous pinch of turmeric
Dash of salt
½ cup converted rice
2½ tablespoons Chinese rice wine vinegar

1 tablespoon vegetable oil
2 tablespoons chopped salted peanuts
2 tablespoons coarsely chopped fresh coriander (cilantro)
Salt and freshly ground pepper

Combine water, turmeric and salt in heavy 1-quart saucepan and bring to boil over medium-high heat. Reduce heat to low, add rice, cover and cook 20 minutes. Remove from heat and let stand, covered, about 5 minutes. Transfer rice to container. Stir in vinegar and oil and let cool. Add remaining ingredients and toss well. Cover and chill.

Southwestern Noodle Salad

An unusual approach to the traditional macaroni salad. Make it two or three days ahead but do taste before serving since it may need a dash more salt and an extra splash of vinegar. Vegetables can be chopped in processor. If chopping by hand, place green pepper (cut into strips), green onions, celery and green chili on a board and cut up all at once. This reduces your chopping time by 75 percent.

12 servings

1 pound medium to small shell macaroni, cooked al dente, thoroughly drained
⅔ cup cider vinegar
¼ cup vegetable oil
1 cup minced celery (about 2 stalks)
½ cup chopped (about ½ large) green pepper
6 green onions, minced
1 2-ounce jar chopped pimientos, drained
3 generous dashes Worcestershire sauce

3 dashes hot pepper sauce
1 tablespoon minced, roasted green chili
1 teaspoon salt
½ teaspoon freshly ground pepper
1 15-ounce can black-eyed peas, drained
1 12-ounce can corn, drained
½ cup pitted black olives, drained and chopped
1 2-ounce jar green olives with pimientos, drained and chopped
⅓ cup mayonnaise (about)

Place macaroni in large bowl. Pour vinegar over and let stand while preparing other ingredients.

Add remaining ingredients to macaroni and mix well. Cover and refrigerate 2 to 3 days. Taste for seasoning before serving. (There should be a suggestion of chili and a tart tang from the vinegar.)

Fettuccine Salad

Salad can be prepared one or two days ahead and tossed just before serving.

2 servings

¼ pound fettuccine egg noodles
¼ cup whipping cream
¼ cup minced fresh parsley
¼ cup freshly grated Parmesan cheese
1 tablespoon olive oil

1 tablespoon white wine vinegar
4 large fresh mushrooms, thinly sliced
1 green onion, thinly sliced
Salt and freshly ground white pepper

Cook noodles in rapidly boiling salted water until al dente. Drain well in colander and then on paper towels to remove as much water as possible. Combine remaining ingredients in large mixing bowl and blend well. Add noodles but do not toss. Cover and chill.

Bring to room temperature and toss lightly just before ready to serve.

Green Pasta Salad

This salad will keep several days stored, covered, in refrigerator. Perfect for outdoor barbecues and picnics.

4 servings

1 pound green noodles
¼ to ½ cup chopped green onion (including tops)
¼ cup Italian dressing
1 2-ounce jar or can chopped pimientos, drained

½ to ¾ cup mayonnaise
½ to ¾ cup sour cream
Salt and freshly ground pepper
½ cup sunflower seed, toasted (optional)

Cook noodles in rapidly boiling water until al dente. Cool quickly under cold running water; drain thoroughly. Transfer to large bowl and toss gently with green onion, dressing and pimientos. Combine equal parts mayonnaise and sour cream and add to pasta with salt and pepper. Toss again, adding sunflower seed just before serving if desired.

Papaya and Potato Salad with Mango Chutney Vinaigrette

Potatoes can be prepared up to two days in advance.

12 servings

2 pounds new potatoes, unpeeled
Mango Chutney Vinaigrette (see following recipe)

Romaine lettuce and grape leaves (garnish)
18 thin slices smoked ham, rolled into cylinders
1 sweet red onion, thinly sliced

3 avocados, peeled, pitted, sliced lengthwise and sprinkled with lemon juice
3 cucumbers, peeled, scored and thinly sliced
2 papayas, peeled, seeded and thinly sliced
16 broccoli florets

Combine potatoes in large saucepan with enough water to cover and bring to boil over medium-high heat. Reduce heat and simmer just until fork tender, about 25 minutes. Drain and cool. Cut into ¼-inch slices. Arrange potato slices in large pan. Cover with Chutney Vinaigrette and toss gently to coat thoroughly. Cover with plastic wrap. Refrigerate up to 2 days.

To serve, drain potatoes, reserving vinaigrette. Cover large serving platter with romaine lettuce and grape leaves. Arrange potatoes, ham, onion, avocado, cucumber, papaya and broccoli over top. Accompany with vinaigrette.

Mango Chutney Vinaigrette

Vinaigrette can be prepared one to two weeks ahead and refrigerated.

Makes about 2 cups

2 mild green chilies (fresh or canned), deveined and seeded
1 cup olive oil
⅓ cup apple cider vinegar
⅓ cup mango chutney (preferably homemade)

1 teaspoon minced garlic
1 teaspoon Dijon mustard
1 teaspoon salt
Freshly ground white pepper

Combine all ingredients in blender or processor and mix well. Season to taste.

Sicilian Orange Salad

Must be prepared ahead and allowed to stand several hours at room temperature before serving.

10 to 12 servings

8 large navel oranges, peeled (remove all white membrane) and thinly sliced

1 medium red onion, sliced into thin rings

½ cup (about) oil-cured black olives
Olive oil
Freshly ground black pepper

Arrange orange slices in overlapping pattern on serving platter. Top with onion rings and olives. Sprinkle lightly with oil and top with generous grinding of pepper.

4 🍏 Entrées

One simple question, asked daily of most cooks, may well be the most perplexing of all words spoken in the kitchen: "What's for dinner?" Keeping main courses interesting from day to day is a difficult challenge for the busy cook. But when so many different and delicious entrées can be made in advance and refrigerated or frozen, you can always be assured of serving exciting meals to your family and friends.

Even poached fish, with its delicate texture and flavor, can sustain up to a day of advance preparation (recipes, pages 34–35). The key to success is in pairing the fish with a complementary sauce that protects it during reheating (see box, page 36).

Main course roasts or grills of poultry or meat do not take well to reheating; but that does not rule them out for some kind of make-ahead strategy. Yogurt Barbecued Chicken (page 44), for example, marinates for two days in a spicy yogurt mixture that makes it remarkably flavorful, moist and tender; it goes straight from its marinade to the hot charcoal grill. And many roasts are excellent cold: The Glazed Cornish Hens on page 47, for example, can be roasted and refrigerated the night before an elegant picnic.

It is no coincidence that many of the dishes in this chapter are braises and stews. They store impeccably in the refrigerator or freezer, and their flavors only get better with reheating. The quantities of a Brunswick Stew (page 45), Spicy Malaysian Lamb (page 60) or New Mexico Chili (page 55) can be doubled easily and the preplanned leftovers frozen for meals months later.

Whatever entrée you prepare, it is helpful to think about taking the recipe step by step. Many elements of a dish—chopped vegetables, for example, or a sauce—can be prepared in advance and stored until ready to use. It also helps to take advantage of the home freezer, stockpiling fresh seasonal herbs, broths, meats, cheeses, fish and poultry. That way, you will always have good quality basic ingredients on hand, ready to turn into tempting main courses at almost a moment's notice.

 Seafood

Fish Fillets in Mustard Sauce

Fillets can be poached and sauced in the morning, reheated before serving.

Set off this tangy offering with thick slices of tomato masked with mayonnaise that has been mixed with some finely chopped onion and Parmesan cheese, then broiled until puffed and golden. Tender green peas and hot buttered rolls followed by fruit and cheese for dessert could round out the menu. Choose a vigorous dry white wine like a Pinot Blanc or Pouilly-Fuissé.

6 servings

6 6- to 7-ounce fish fillets	1 tablespoon dry mustard
1 cup chicken broth	1 cup whipping cream
Salt and freshly ground pepper	4 to 6 teaspoons Dijon mustard
2 tablespoons (¼ stick) butter	Salt and freshly ground pepper
1 tablespoon flour	

Preheat oven to 400°F. Pat fish dry with paper towels. Place in single layer in two 9 × 13-inch baking dishes. Pour broth over and sprinkle with salt and pepper. Bake covered 10 to 15 minutes, or until fish loses its translucency. Transfer cooked fillets to platter.

Pour poaching liquid into small saucepan and bring to boil over high heat. Continue cooking until liquid has reduced to ¾ cup.

Melt butter in medium skillet over medium heat. Add flour and dry mustard and cook, stirring constantly, 2 minutes. Remove from heat and add reduced liquid, stirring until smooth and well blended.

Combine cream with Dijon mustard and stir into sauce. Return to burner and stir until thickened. Add salt and pepper to taste. Return fillets to baking dish and cover with sauce. *Dish may be covered and refrigerated up to this point. Remove from refrigerator and let stand 2 hours before reheating.*

Just before serving, preheat oven to 400°F. Bake uncovered 6 to 8 minutes, or until sauce is bubbly and fish is heated through.

Sherry-Poached Fish with Oranges

This dish can be assembled hours in advance and reheated before serving.

Serve with rice pilaf; fresh spinach salad with crumbled bacon, chopped red onion and cucumber slices; hot biscuits and a soft, rounded wine like a Johannisberg Riesling or a Chenin Blanc.

6 servings

6 6- to 7-ounce fish fillets	2 green onions, minced
Salt	½ cup whipping cream
½ cup dry Sherry	2 tablespoons orange juice
3 tablespoons butter	Slivered zest of 1 orange

Preheat oven to 400°F. Pat fish dry with paper towels. Place in single layer in two 9 × 13-inch baking dishes. Sprinkle with salt and cover with Sherry. Bake covered 10 to 15 minutes, or until fish loses its translucency. Transfer fillets to platter. Pour liquid into saucepan and reduce over medium-high heat to ⅔ cup.

Melt butter in small saucepan over medium heat. Add onion and sauté until limp. Remove from heat and stir in reserved poaching liquid, cream, orange juice and zest. Return to burner, bring to simmer over low heat and cook 5 minutes, stirring frequently. Cool. Return fillets to baking dish and cover with sauce. *Dish may be covered and refrigerated at this point. Remove from refrigerator 2 hours before reheating.*

Just before serving, preheat oven to 400°F. Bake covered 8 to 10 minutes, or until sauce is bubbly.

If thicker sauce is preferred, dissolve 1 to 2 tablespoons flour in small amount of whipping cream in small saucepan or heatproof dish over low heat. Stir into sauce, return to burner and bring to simmer, stirring occasionally, until sauce is desired consistency.

Poached Salmon with Sorrel Sauce

The fish and sauce can be prepared ahead and refrigerated, then reheated before serving.

Because of its fresh, slightly tangy flavor, sorrel is an ideal companion for salmon. Serve with a chilled dry Sauvignon Blanc or a Fumé Blanc.

6 servings

6 1¼-inch thick salmon fillets
1 cup dry white wine
¾ cup clam juice or fish stock
¼ cup dry vermouth

3 tablespoons butter
½ pound fresh sorrel, washed, drained and shredded, or ¼ to ½ cup canned sorrel, well drained

5 tablespoons butter
1 tablespoon finely chopped shallot
½ cup whipping cream
Salt and freshly ground pepper

Preheat oven to 400°F. Pat fish dry with paper towels. Place in single layer in two 9 × 13-inch baking dishes. Combine wine, juice or stock, and vermouth and pour over fillets. Bake covered 10 to 15 minutes, or until fish loses its translucency. Transfer fillets to platter. Reserve liquid for sauce.

Melt 3 tablespoons butter in small skillet over medium heat. Add fresh sorrel a handful at a time, stirring well after each addition, or add canned sorrel all at once. With fresh sorrel, reduce heat, cover and simmer 10 minutes or until tender, stirring occasionally; just heat through if using canned. Drain well, transfer to food processor or blender and puree.

Melt 1 tablespoon butter in small saucepan over medium heat. Add shallot and sauté briefly. Stir in reserved liquid, increase heat and boil vigorously until reduced by ½. Remove from heat and add cream. Return to burner and simmer until sauce has thickened slightly. Add sorrel puree to taste and stir until well blended. Remove from heat and gradually add remaining 4 tablespoons butter a little at a time, mixing well after each addition. Season with salt and pepper. Return fillets to baking dish and cover with sauce. *Dish may be covered and refrigerated at this point. Remove from refrigerator 2 hours before reheating.*

Just before serving, preheat oven to 350°F. Bake covered 15 to 20 minutes, or until sauce is bubbly and fish is heated through.

Poached Fish Provençale

This piquant red snapper can be prepared ahead and refrigerated. Reheat and garnish before serving.

6 servings

6 6- to 7-ounce red snapper fillets
   Salt and freshly ground pepper
1 cup light-bodied red wine

2 tablespoons (¼ stick) butter
¼ cup chopped onion
2 garlic cloves, minced
3 tablespoons tomato sauce
2 tablespoons minced fresh parsley
¼ teaspoon oregano

¼ teaspoon thyme
¼ teaspoon rosemary
½ teaspoon arrowroot dissolved in 1 tablespoon cold water

Black olives (garnish)
Minced fresh parsley (garnish)

Preheat oven to 400°F. Pat fish dry with paper towels. Place in single layer in two 9 × 13-inch baking dishes. Sprinkle with salt and pepper and cover with wine. Bake covered 10 to 15 minutes, or until fish loses its translucency. Transfer fillets to platter. Measure liquid. If there is more than 1 cup, boil to reduce; if there is less than 1 cup, add additional wine to correct measurement.

Melt butter in medium skillet over medium heat. Add onion and sauté until almost transparent. Add garlic and cook until lightly golden. Stir in reserved liquid, tomato sauce, 2 tablespoons parsley, oregano, thyme and rosemary and blend well. Increase heat and bring sauce to boil, stirring constantly. Reduce heat to simmer, blend in arrowroot and continue stirring until sauce has thickened. Taste and adjust seasoning if necessary. Return fillets to baking dish and cover with sauce. *Dish may be covered and refrigerated at this point. Remove from refrigerator 2 hours before reheating.*

Just before serving, preheat oven to 350°F. Bake covered 15 to 18 minutes, or until heated through. Garnish with olives and a sprinkling of parsley.

❧ *Do-Ahead Poached Fish*

It's possible to serve a perfectly poached fish and to do it in simple make-ahead steps. In the morning the fish is oven-poached with a little wine or other liquid, which is drained off and used as a basis for the sauce. The sauce is then spooned over the fish before it is covered and refrigerated. When the fish is ready to be reheated the sauce will mask and protect its delicate flavor and juices. It's best to bring the fish to room temperature by removing the dish from the refrigerator about two hours before reheating. For a more elegant presentation, complete the first baking in a shallow pan, then transfer the fish to individual au gratin dishes before adding the sauce.

To choose the best fish for this treatment, consider what is freshest in your own market. Examine as possible candidates not just familiar sole (actually what is called sole in this country may be flounder, dab, lemon sole or gray sole—all delicious), but also haddock, whitefish, salmon, hake (whiting), swordfish, pompano, pollock, grouper, yellowtail, cusk, cod, trout, ocean perch, red snapper, brill, rockfish, butterfish or turbot.

Fresh fish is always preferable to frozen. Fresh fillets should be firm and elastic to the touch. Any sign of mushiness is a signal for rejection. Try to buy fish just before coming home or use a cold chest or a heavy duty plastic bag with ice to refrigerate it if there will be a long delay.

If you live far from a river or ocean, you'll have to rely on frozen fish. It's much more difficult to judge the quality of frozen fillets since the packaging often covers up too much. However, be sure to choose a package that's firmly frozen and keep it at −5°F or colder until you are ready to cook it. Thaw fish slowly in the refrigerator—fillets will thaw overnight. Buy one pound whole fish or ⅓ to ½ pound of fillet per person.

It's easier to buy fish that has already been filleted, but you may want to learn to do it yourself. If anyone with a rod and reel and a generous turn of mind inhabits your neighborhood, fish filleting could be a very useful skill.

To oven-poach your fish, place the fillets or steaks in a shallow buttered baking pan and pour over the liquid suggested for the particular recipe. Cover with foil or buttered waxed paper and place in a preheated oven. Count on cooking the fish slightly less than 10 minutes per inch of thickness (measured at the thickest point) from the time the liquid reaches a boil. Make the sauce as directed and spoon it over the cooked fish. When ready to serve, reheat the fish. You may want to run it under the broiler for a moment after reheating; in some cases, this could affect the texture of the sauce.

It will be fish as you like it—succulent, moist, tender and nestled under a sauce created to enhance the best of your catch.

Spinach Sole with Pesto Sauce

This dish can be prepared in advance and reheated before serving.

The sunny Italian flavor of the pesto-touched sauce combines well with rata-touille, crusty French or Italian bread, crisp green salad and a strong, dry white wine like a Pinot Blanc or a Pouilly-Fuissé.

6 servings

6 6- to 7-ounce sole fillets
  Salt and freshly ground pepper
1 cup dry white vermouth
1 tablespoon fresh lemon juice

2 tablespoons (¼ stick) butter
¼ cup chopped onion
1 garlic clove, minced
1 10-ounce package frozen chopped spinach, thawed and very well drained

¾ cup freshly grated Parmesan cheese
½ teaspoon oregano
  Salt and freshly ground pepper

1 cup sour cream
¼ cup pesto sauce (available dried or frozen)
  Salt and freshly ground pepper

Preheat oven to 400°F. Pat fish dry with paper towels. Place in single layer in two 9 × 13-inch baking dishes. Sprinkle with salt and pepper and cover with vermouth and lemon juice. Bake covered 10 to 15 minutes, or until fish loses its translucency. Pour off liquid and reserve. Remove fish and set aside to cool. Pour liquid into saucepan and reduce over medium-high heat to ½ cup.

Meanwhile, melt butter in medium skillet over moderate heat. Add onion and garlic and sauté until just golden. Turn into bowl. Add spinach, ¼ cup Parmesan, oregano, salt and pepper and mix well (it will be quite thick). Return fillets to baking dishes. Divide spinach mixture over each, spreading evenly.

Add sour cream and pesto sauce to reduced liquid. Season to taste with salt and pepper. Spoon mixture over fillets and sprinkle with remaining Parmesan. *Dish may be covered and refrigerated at this point. Remove from refrigerator 2 hours before reheating.*

Just before serving, preheat oven to 350°F. Bake uncovered 5 to 10 minutes, or until heated through, then run under broiler several minutes, until cheese is melted and bubbly.

Poisson d'Avril en Papillote
(Fillet of Sole with Brandy-Champagne Sauce)

Surprise your guests with this fillet of sole, topped with a Brandy-Champagne Sauce, surrounded by colorful vegetables and baked en papillote.

Sauce and vegetables can be prepared ahead and refrigerated. Vegetables are glazed just before fillets en papillote are assembled and baked.

8 servings

8 10-inch squares of parchment paper

4 cups (1 quart) water
¼ cup fresh lemon juice
24 small fresh sole fillets

6 cups chicken stock
2 large turnips, peeled and cut into 1 × 2-inch ovals
8 pearl onions
8 small carrots, cut into 1 × 2-inch ovals
1 pound fresh green beans, cut into 2-inch pieces

Brandy-Champagne Sauce
½ cup (1 stick) butter
½ cup all purpose flour

2 cups Fast and Easy Fish Stock (see following recipe)
1 cup Champagne or sparkling dry white wine

2 tablespoons (¼ stick) butter
2 cups small mushroom caps
1 cup whipping cream
2 tablespoons brandy
  Salt and freshly ground pepper

Vegetable Glaze
3 tablespoons water
2 tablespoons (¼ stick) butter
¼ teaspoon sugar
¼ teaspoon salt

2 egg whites, lightly beaten

Fold each piece of paper in half and cut out large heart shape. Set aside.

Combine water and lemon juice in large bowl. Dip each fillet into water; drain well. Cover and refrigerate.

Bring chicken stock to boil in 4-quart saucepan over high heat. Add turnips and onions and blanch 2 minutes. Remove with slotted spoon and plunge into cold water to stop cooking process; drain well. Pat dry with paper towels. Transfer to bowl. Repeat with carrots (blanching 3 minutes) and beans (blanching 4 minutes). Vegetables should be barely fork tender and retain color. *(Vegetables can be prepared ahead to this point and refrigerated.)*

For sauce: Melt ½ cup (1 stick) butter in 2-quart saucepan over medium heat. When butter is foamy, add flour and stir until roux is bubbly, about 1 to 2 minutes. Add fish stock and Champagne and simmer until sauce is reduced to consistency of whipping cream, about 5 to 10 minutes.

Melt 2 tablespoons butter in 10-inch skillet over medium heat. Add mushroom caps and sauté 2 to 3 minutes. Add to sauce using slotted spoon. Stir in cream, brandy, salt and pepper and bring to simmer. Set aside and keep warm. *(Sauce can be prepared ahead to this point and refrigerated.)*

For glaze: Stir water, butter, sugar and salt in medium skillet over low heat. Add vegetables, shaking pan constantly, until well glazed, about 3 to 4 minutes. Remove from heat.

Preheat oven to 375°F. Roll up fillets and set 3 on upper half of 1 parchment paper heart. Arrange vegetables around fish. Pour some of sauce over top. (Pass any remaining sauce when serving.) Fold bottom of heart over fish; fold edges over to seal. Fold tip of heart several times to seal. Brush top of packet with egg white. Repeat with remaining fillets. Transfer to baking sheet(s). Bake until paper is golden brown, about 10 minutes.

Fast and Easy Fish Stock

Stock can be prepared ahead and frozen.

Makes 6 to 7 cups

4 8-ounce bottles clam juice	1 onion, halved
4 cups (1 quart) water	2 carrots, cut into 2-inch pieces
2 cups dry white wine	3 parsley sprigs
1 lemon, thinly sliced and seeded	
1 celery stalk (with leaves), cut into 2-inch pieces	

Bring clam juice, water, wine, lemon, vegetables and parsley to boil in 4- to 5-quart saucepan over high heat. Reduce heat and simmer until liquid is reduced to 6 to 7 cups.

Latticed Lobster Tart

Tart can be assembled ahead and frozen one to two days. Brush with beaten egg and bake before serving.

4 to 6 servings

2 tablespoons (¼ stick) unsalted butter	⅓ cup sour cream
1 1-pound lobster, boiled, shell discarded, meat finely chopped, or ½ pound cooked crabmeat or ½ pound boiled, shelled shrimp	1 tablespoon chopped fresh dill or 1 teaspoon dried dillweed
Ground red pepper	½ pound Whole Wheat Puff Pastry (see following recipe)
2 tablespoons dry Sherry	1 egg, beaten
1 tablespoon whole wheat pastry flour	

Melt butter in medium skillet over low heat. Add lobster and sprinkle with ground red pepper. Cook until warmed through, about 1 to 2 minutes. Remove from heat. Warm Sherry in small saucepan over medium-high heat. Remove from heat, ignite and pour over lobster. Sprinkle lobster with flour. Stir in sour cream and dill. Transfer mixture to bowl and let cool; refrigerate.

Turn dough out onto lightly floured surface and roll into large rectangle about ⅛ inch thick. Cut into 2 equal rectangles. Transfer one rectangle to dampened baking sheet and set aside. Fold remaining rectangle in half lengthwise. Cut ½-inch strips along folded side to within ½ inch of open edge.

Brush edges of uncut pastry rectangle with water. Spread lobster mixture down center. Unfold cut rectangle and set over lobster mixture, aligning with bottom edges. Press edges together to seal. Chill tart in freezer at least 30 minutes. *(Lobster Tart can be prepared ahead to this point and frozen 1 to 2 days.)*

Preheat oven to 400°F. Brush chilled tart with beaten egg. Bake until golden brown, about 30 minutes.

Whole Wheat Puff Pastry

This pastry can be made ahead and frozen but is best prepared and baked the same day.

Makes 1 pound

2 cups stoneground whole wheat bread flour
½ teaspoon sea salt
⅓ cup plus 2 tablespoons ice-cold water or well-chilled nonfat milk

2 teaspoons fresh lemon juice
1¼ cups (2½ sticks) unsalted butter, chilled and cut into ½-inch cubes

Combine 1¾ cups flour and salt in processor and mix using 1 to 2 on/off turns. With machine running, add water or milk and lemon juice and mix until dough forms ball, about 2 to 3 minutes. Turn dough out onto *unfloured* surface and shape into smooth ball. Make deep crosscut on top of ball using sharp knife. Cover with plastic wrap and chill in freezer until firm, about 30 minutes.

Meanwhile, combine butter and remaining flour in large bowl and mix until smooth. Turn out onto surface. Form into 4-inch square using spatula. Cover butter with plastic wrap and chill in freezer until firm, about 20 minutes.

When dough and butter are chilled to equal firmness but not frozen, transfer dough to lightly floured surface and roll into 12-inch square. Set butter mixture in center of dough and fold sides over butter evenly, making sure ends meet in center. Pinch ends of dough together so there are no holes. Using rolling pin, make series of slight depressions in crisscross pattern over dough until square is flattened to 8 inches. Roll dough into rectangle. Fold top ⅓ toward center; fold remaining ⅓ over top, as for business letter. *This is called a single turn.* Cover with plastic wrap and chill in freezer until firm but not frozen, about 20 minutes.

Turn dough out onto lightly floured surface with open end toward you. Roll into large rectangle about ⅜ inch thick. Fold short ends so they meet at center of dough without overlapping. Fold dough in half at center. *This is called a double turn.* Cover dough with plastic wrap and chill in freezer until firm but not frozen, about 20 minutes.

Repeat single turn, chilling in freezer until firm but not frozen, about 20 minutes. Repeat double turn *three* more times, chilling in freezer after each. Cover with plastic and refrigerate.

Swiss Enchiladas with Lobster and Shrimp

Swiss Enchiladas can be prepared several hours in advance and held in luke-warm (180°F) oven. They also freeze well. Defrost in refrigerator overnight before reheating.

12 servings

12 to 16 corn tortillas
2 medium white onions, coarsely chopped
1 7-ounce can green chilies, membranes discarded, coarsely chopped
1½ pounds frozen lobster tails, thawed and coarsely chopped
1 pound uncooked large shrimp, peeled and deveined, coarsely chopped
1 cup walnut halves, toasted
1 12-ounce can medium or large pitted ripe olives, well drained, halved

1 pound Monterey Jack cheese, shredded
1 pound longhorn cheddar cheese, shredded

2 cups half and half
1 cup sour cream
½ cup (1 stick) butter, melted
1½ teaspoons oregano leaves
1 teaspoon garlic salt

Shredded longhorn cheddar cheese (optional)
Sliced red pimientos, avocado slices, sliced black or green olives (optional garnish)

Preheat oven to 300°F. Generously butter large *cazuela* (Mexican casserole dish) or deep 4-quart casserole.

Cover bottom with about ⅓ of tortillas. Sprinkle with half of onion and top with half of chilies. Add half of lobster and shrimp. Sprinkle with half of walnuts and half of olives. Combine Jack and cheddar cheeses; remove about 1½ cups and set aside. Sprinkle half of remaining cheese over olives.

Combine half and half, sour cream, butter, oregano and garlic salt in medium saucepan. Place over medium-low heat and stir frequently until lukewarm and well blended. Remove 1 cup and set aside. Pour half of remaining sauce over casserole. Repeat layering, covering top with remaining half of sauce. Add remaining tortillas, 1 cup reserved sauce and ¾ cup of the reserved cheese.

Bake 60 to 75 minutes, until casserole is bubbling hot. Remove from oven and increase temperature to 450°F. Sprinkle casserole with remaining cheese and return to oven for 5 to 7 minutes, until top is golden brown and cheese is bubbly. If using optional garnish add more cheddar and return to oven just until cheese is melted. Alternate pimientos, avocado slices and olives in wagonwheel design and heat briefly until toppings begin to sink into cheese.

Other shellfish or cooked chicken may be substituted for lobster and shrimp. Recipe can be doubled or tripled.

Deviled Crab

This dish can be assembled one day ahead. Cover and refrigerate until ready to bake.

10 to 12 servings

2 pounds Dungeness crabmeat, rinsed and drained
2 cups salted cracker crumbs (measure by breaking crackers into large chunks using hands)
1 cup finely diced celery
¾ cup chopped onion
2 tablespoons chopped fresh parsley

1 tablespoon chopped green pepper
1½ teaspoons dry mustard
½ teaspoon salt
4 drops hot pepper sauce or to taste
Dash of ground red pepper
¾ cup (1½ sticks) butter, melted
¾ cup whipping cream, half and half or milk

Preheat oven to 350°F. Combine first 4 ingredients in large mixing bowl and blend well. Add parsley, green pepper, mustard, salt, hot pepper sauce and red pepper and mix thoroughly. Stir in butter and cream. Turn into shallow 3-quart casserole. Cover and bake until bubbly, about 30 minutes.

Recipe can be doubled.

Fresh Basil Pesto with pasta

Terrine Maison with Cumberland Sauce

Cabbage Borscht

Veal and Sorrel Stew in Gougère Ring,
Goulash with Wine-Braised Sauerkraut

Jambon Chaud-Froid

Basic Croissants

Scandinavian Seafood Stew

Vegetable-stock mixture can be prepared one day ahead and refrigerated. Heat with seafood before serving.

This full-flavored dish needs only a green salad, Swedish rye bread and a dry Chablis to make a party dinner.

8 servings

1 pound tiny onions, peeled*
2 large leeks (white part only), cleaned and chopped
2 medium carrots, finely chopped
3 tablespoons butter
1 teaspoon dried thyme or 1 tablespoon fresh
1 teaspoon dried dillweed or 1 tablespoon minced fresh dill
¼ teaspoon dried savory or ¾ teaspoon minced fresh
Generous pinch of ground cardamom
1½ pounds new potatoes, peeled and cut into small cubes
7 cups Spiced Fish Stock (see following recipe)

½ cup whipping cream

1½ pounds clams or mussels, soaked in cold water with 1 teaspoon salt for 1 hour, rinsed, scrubbed and debearded
1 pound medium shrimp, shelled and deveined
1 pound cod fillet, cut into bite-size pieces
1 pound haddock fillet, cut into bite-size pieces
¼ to ½ teaspoon salt
¼ teaspoon freshly ground pepper
½ cup minced green onion tops (garnish)
1 tablespoon minced fresh dill (optional garnish)

Combine onions, leek, carrot, butter, herbs and cardamom in heavy, nonaluminum 6-quart pan. Cover and cook over low heat until vegetables are wilted, about 20 minutes. Add potato and stock and simmer until onions and potato are tender. *(Can be prepared a day in advance up to this point and chilled.)*

About 15 minutes before serving, bring to gentle simmer. Stir in cream. Add clams or mussels, cover and cook very gently until shells *begin* to open. Add shrimp and cook until barely firm, about 1 minute longer. Stir in cod and haddock and season with salt and pepper. Ladle into bowls. *(Do not allow the fish to overcook, as it continues to cook in the stock.)* Discard any clams or mussels that have not opened and sprinkle each serving with some of the onion tops and dill. Serve immediately.

*For ease in peeling tiny onions, drop them into boiling water and boil one minute. Drain in colander. Rinse with cold water until cool, then trim off tops and bottoms. Make a slit in skin and slip off.

Spiced Fish Stock

Stock can be made one or two days ahead and refrigerated, or frozen up to three months.

This recipe produces a more robust stock than most. Store trimmings in the freezer until five or six pounds have accumulated, then make stock.

Makes about 3 quarts

5 to 6 pounds fish trimmings (bones, heads, tails), preferably from white-fleshed fish (thaw if frozen)
2 large onions, sliced
1 large carrot, sliced
26 whole white peppercorns
4 unpeeled garlic cloves
4 whole allspice berries
3 whole cardamom pods

2 parsley sprigs
1 whole clove
½ teaspoon dried thyme
Salt
1 bottle (750 ml) dry white wine (Fumé Blanc, Chardonnay or Chablis)
2 quarts (8 cups) water

Place fish trimmings in heavy, nonaluminum 8-quart pan. Sprinkle with onion, carrot, peppercorns, garlic, allspice, cardamom, parsley, clove, thyme and salt. Cover and cook over medium-low heat until fish has released its juices, about 15 minutes, watching carefully to avoid burning. Add wine and water and slowly bring to simmer, skimming off any foam that rises to surface. Partially cover and simmer gently 45 minutes. Strain through several layers of dampened cheesecloth.

 Poultry

Chicken Fricassee with Spring Vegetables

Chicken and vegetables can be prepared ahead and refrigerated. Sauce is made just before serving.

4 servings

1½ pounds asparagus (tips cut off diagonally and reserved), stems trimmed, peeled and cut diagonally into 1½-inch pieces
1 cucumber, peeled, halved, seeded and cut into balls with small melon baller
  Peel of 2 lemons, cut into ⅛-inch julienne
1 cup shelled fava beans (1 pound unshelled) or ¼ pound green beans, trimmed

3 tablespoons unsalted butter
1 small leek (white part only), thinly sliced
1 cup shelled fresh peas (1 pound unshelled)
  Pinch of sugar (optional)
1 tablespoon fresh lemon juice
  Salt and freshly ground pepper

2 tablespoons (¼ stick) butter

2 tablespoons oil
1 2½- to 3-pound chicken, cut up and patted dry
  Salt and freshly ground pepper
1 tablespoon minced fresh tarragon or 1 teaspoon dried, crumbled
1 bay leaf
1 cup dry white wine or vermouth
3 cups (about) chicken stock, preferably homemade

6 egg yolks, room temperature
1 cup whipping cream
1 tablespoon fresh lemon juice

1 tablespoon butter
1 tablespoon *each* minced fresh parsley, chervil and tarragon (garnish)
4 fluted lemon slices (garnish)

Bring large pot of salted water to boil over medium-high heat. Add asparagus pieces and cook until almost tender when pierced with knife, about 3 to 5 minutes. Add tips and cook until tender, about 2 minutes. Remove with slotted spoon and plunge into ice water to stop cooking process. Pat dry with paper towels. Repeat with cucumber, cooking about 2 minutes; lemon peel, cooking about 10 minutes; and fava beans, cooking about 5 minutes (4 minutes for green beans). Remove husks from fava beans and discard.

Melt 3 tablespoons butter in medium skillet over low heat. Add leek, cover and let sweat 15 minutes, stirring occasionally. Add peas, cover and cook 10 minutes. Add sugar if desired. Stir in fava beans and cook until vegetables are tender, about 5 minutes. Remove from heat. Add asparagus, cucumber and lemon juice. Season to taste.

Preheat oven to 325°F. Heat 2 tablespoons butter with oil in large skillet over medium-high heat. Add chicken and sauté on all sides until lightly browned. Sprinkle with salt and pepper. Transfer chicken to heatproof baking dish, arranging white meat on top. Add tarragon, bay leaf, wine and enough stock to cover chicken completely. Partially cover dish, place over low heat and bring to simmer. Cover and bake 15 minutes. Remove white meat and bake remaining pieces 5 minutes longer. Transfer chicken to platter using slotted spoon and set aside.

Discard fat from dish. Place over medium-high heat and cook until liquid is reduced to 2 cups. Add chicken. *(Chicken and vegetables can be made ahead to this point and refrigerated.)*

Place dish over medium-low heat and bring mixture to simmer. When chicken is heated through, transfer to serving plate. Tent with foil.

Whisk egg yolks and cream in large bowl. Slowly whisk heated stock into yolk mixture, then return to dish. Place over medium heat and stir with wooden spoon until mixture thickens and finger drawn across coated spoon leaves a path; *do not boil, or yolks will curdle.* Stir in lemon juice and season mixture with salt and pepper to taste.

Melt 1 tablespoon butter in medium saucepan over medium-high heat. Add vegetables and reheat. Divide chicken and sauce evenly among heated soup plates. Spoon vegetables over chicken. Sprinkle with parsley, chervil and tarragon. Garnish with lemon peel and fluted lemon slices. Serve immediately.

Escabeche

This dish is best when prepared one day ahead.

6 servings

- 2 3-pound chickens, cut into serving pieces
- ½ cup olive oil
- 2 cups dry white wine
- 2 cups cider vinegar
- 2 cups hot water
- 6 carrots, sliced diagonally ⅛ inch thick
- 4 medium onions, cut into eighths
- 4 celery stalks, sliced
- 2 small leeks (including some of green tops), sliced
  Bouquet garni (4 parsley sprigs, 1 bay leaf, 2 to 3 whole cloves and ½ teaspoon thyme)
  Salt and freshly ground pepper
- 2 lemons, thinly sliced (garnish)

Pat chicken dry with paper towels. Heat oil in heavy 6- to 8-quart Dutch oven or stockpot. Add chicken in batches and brown well on all sides. Pour off fat and return chicken to pot. Add remaining ingredients except lemons and bring to boil over high heat. Reduce heat to medium-low, cover and simmer gently until chicken is tender, about 30 minutes. Remove from heat and let chicken cool to room temperature in stock.

Discard bouquet garni. Remove skin and bones from chicken and cut meat into finger-size pieces. Remove vegetables. Cool broth; discard fat and strain broth through cheesecloth. Pour small amount of broth into large, deep serving bowl. Arrange chicken in spoke pattern in bottom. Top with carrot slices in overlapping pattern. Distribute onion wedges, leeks and ⅔ of celery around outer edge. Top carrot with remaining ⅓ of celery. Pour remaining broth over vegetables. Refrigerate until set. Just before serving, twist lemon slices and place along outer edge.

Perkedel Ayam (Chicken Fritters with Shallots and Garlic)

Fritters can be fried ahead and frozen. Thaw at room temperature one hour, then reheat in 400°F oven or run under broiler.

Makes about 25

- 2 teaspoons butter
- 4 medium shallots, thinly sliced
- 1 garlic clove, thinly sliced
- ½ teaspoon salt
- ½ teaspoon freshly ground pepper
- ¼ teaspoon freshly grated nutmeg
- 2 cups cubed skinned, boned chicken breast (about 1 pound)
- 2 eggs
- 2 teaspoons cornstarch
- ¼ cup peanut oil or corn oil

Melt butter in heavy large skillet over medium heat. Add shallot and garlic and sauté 2 minutes. Stir in salt, pepper and nutmeg, blending well. Set aside.

Coarsely puree chicken in processor. Add eggs, cornstarch and shallot mixture and blend well. Heat oil in wok or heavy large skillet over medium-high heat. Add chicken mixture to oil by heaping teaspoons (do not crowd) and brown on both sides, 2 to 3 minutes. Remove with slotted spoon; drain on paper towel. Repeat with remaining chicken mixture. Transfer to platter and serve immediately.

Yogurt Barbecued Chicken

Chicken is marinated two days before grilling. The marinade works equally well with roasted turkey breast, pork or beef.

4 to 6 servings

1 cup plain yogurt (homemade or commercial)
¼ cup firmly packed dark brown sugar
4 large garlic cloves
3 tablespoons cider vinegar

2 teaspoons Worcestershire sauce
2 dashes hot pepper sauce
1 3-pound chicken, cut into 8 pieces

Combine all ingredients except chicken in food processor or blender and mix until smooth. Arrange chicken in single layer in shallow dish and pour marinade evenly over top. Cover and refrigerate 48 hours, turning occasionally.

Prepare charcoal grill. Remove chicken from marinade and pat dry with paper towels. Grill over slow fire for about 1 hour, turning often and basting frequently with marinade.

Macédoine of Vegetables with Brown Rice and Chicken

Cooked brown rice can be frozen. Thaw at room temperature or in steamer. Macédoine can be prepared up to three days ahead, covered and refrigerated.

The full-flavored natural brown rice with fresh vegetables and nuts is an especially satisfying main dish. Shredded meat or sliced shrimp can be substituted for the chicken.

4 to 6 servings

¾ cup long-grain natural brown rice
1 egg, beaten
2 cups water or chicken stock
1½ teaspoons light vegetable oil (preferably cold-pressed safflower)
1 teaspoon herb or vegetable salt

2 medium-size ripe tomatoes, peeled, halved, seeded and thinly sliced

¾ cup thinly sliced green onion
¼ cup chopped fresh parsley
¼ cup pine nuts, toasted
1 cup cooked cubed chicken
½ cup Lemon Dressing (see following recipe)
8 to 10 romaine or iceberg lettuce leaves

Preheat oven to 350°F. Combine rice and half of egg in heavy 1-quart saucepan and stir until rice is moistened. Place over medium heat and stir until rice is dry and grains are separate. Add water, oil and herb salt and bring to boil, stirring constantly. Remove from heat. Cover and bake until rice is tender and liquid is absorbed, about 40 minutes (do not stir). Fluff with fork.

Transfer rice to large bowl. Add tomatoes, green onion, parsley and pine nuts and toss lightly. Add chicken and dressing and toss again. Cover and refrigerate until ready to serve. Just before serving, arrange lettuce leaves on plates and spoon rice and chicken mixture over top.

Lemon Dressing

Makes ½ cup

¼ cup fresh lemon juice
3 tablespoons light vegetable oil (preferably cold-pressed safflower)
1 teaspoon herb or vegetable salt
½ teaspoon finely chopped garlic

¼ teaspoon dried marjoram, crumbled
¼ teaspoon dried oregano, crumbled
¼ teaspoon freshly ground pepper

Combine all ingredients in jar with tight-fitting lid and shake well.

Brunswick Stew with Corn Dumplings

Most of the recipe can be prepared several days ahead and refrigerated. This stew is best if it is made with a flavorful stewing hen. Corn Dumplings round out the dish.

8 servings

18 white peppercorns, bruised
6 whole cloves
2 garlic cloves
2 bay leaves
3 sprigs parsley
¼ teaspoon dried thyme or 4 sprigs fresh
2 quarts flavorful chicken stock
1 5- to 6-pound stewing hen or large roaster, quartered (giblets removed and reserved)
1 large onion, chopped

½ pound best quality country bacon, chopped
3 medium onions, chopped

3 medium new potatoes, peeled and cubed
1 1-pound 12-ounce can peeled tomatoes, undrained
1 cup dried baby lima beans, soaked overnight in cold water and drained
2 tablespoons tomato paste
1 whole dried red pepper (optional)
½ teaspoon salt
⅛ teaspoon freshly ground pepper

1 cup fresh okra, halved*
2 cups fresh corn kernels*
Corn Dumplings (see following recipe)

Combine first 6 ingredients in small piece of cheesecloth and secure with string. Add to 8-quart pot with stock and bring to simmer over medium-high heat. Add hen, giblets and 1 chopped onion. Simmer covered until chicken is tender, about 1½ to 2 hours. Chill overnight if desired. Skim fat from surface of stock. Remove chicken; discard skin and bones and cut meat into bite-size pieces. Set aside.

Cook bacon until crisp in medium skillet over medium heat. Remove with slotted spoon to paper towel and drain well. Add to stock. Pour off all but 2 tablespoons fat and place skillet over high heat. Add remaining onion and sauté quickly until browned. Add to stock along with potatoes, tomatoes, lima beans, tomato paste, red pepper, salt and pepper and stir to combine. Cover partially and simmer until beans are tender, about 40 to 60 minutes. *(Stew can be prepared several days ahead to this point and refrigerated.)*

Stir in reserved chicken, okra and corn. Bring stew to simmer, then drop dumpling batter in by tablespoon. Cover pot securely and simmer until dumplings are puffed and a toothpick inserted in center comes out clean, about 15 minutes. Turn stew into soup tureen to serve or spoon dumplings into heated bowls and ladle stew over.

*If fresh okra and corn are not available, frozen vegetables can be substituted. Add to stew when dumplings are done and cook just until heated through.

Corn Dumplings

1 cup all purpose flour
1 tablespoon yellow cornmeal
2 teaspoons baking powder
½ teaspoon salt
Generous pinch of sugar

1 tablespoon butter, chilled
⅓ cup fresh corn kernels or frozen, thawed
⅔ cup cold milk

Combine flour, cornmeal, baking powder, salt and sugar in medium bowl and mix well. Cut in butter using a pastry blender or two knives until mixture resembles coarse meal. Stir in corn using fork, then add milk and stir just until moistened; *do not overmix.* Add to stew and cook as directed.

Chicken and Corn Pot Pie

This delicious variation on an old American favorite can be completely assembled 24 hours before baking. Use fresh corn when available. Country smoked bacon is strongly recommended since regular bacon tends to lose much of its flavor in a dish of this sort. Although this special bacon involves mail-order purchase in most cases, it will keep in the freezer several months. It usually has less shrinkage than the supermarket variety and gives a wonderful aroma and body.

6 servings

1 pound small boiling onions
2 tablespoons (¼ stick) butter
¼ pound slab or country smoked bacon, diced
1 3-pound chicken, quartered
Flour
2 large carrots, diced
1¼ cups rich chicken stock
3 whole cloves
2 whole cardamom pods

½ teaspoon rosemary, crumbled
Salt and freshly ground pepper
½ pound fresh or frozen corn kernels
Cornmeal-Chive Pastry (see recipe, page 90) or **Rough Puff Pastry** (see recipe, page 91)
1 egg, beaten

Bring 1 quart water to boil in saucepan. Add onions and blanch 2 minutes. Drain in colander and rinse thoroughly with cold water. Trim off tops and bottoms of onions and slip off skins.

Melt butter in large, shallow casserole over medium heat. Add bacon and cook until crisp. Remove with slotted spoon and set aside. Lightly dredge chicken pieces in flour. Increase heat as necessary and brown on all sides. Remove chicken and pour off all but 3 tablespoons fat. Add carrot and onions and cook about 3 minutes over medium heat. Add stock, seasonings, chicken and bacon. Bring to gentle simmer, then cover and cook until chicken is tender, about 30 minutes.

Remove chicken and set aside to cool. Skim off fat and reduce sauce over high heat until flavor is rich and intense. Season to taste with salt and pepper. Meanwhile, remove skin and bone from chicken and cut meat into bite-size chunks. Transfer to bowl and add sauce. Cover and refrigerate overnight.

Position rack in center of oven and preheat to 400°F. Generously grease 6-cup soufflé dish. Stir corn into chicken mixture and blend well. Turn into prepared dish. Roll out pastry on floured surface to thickness of ⅛ inch. Cut circle slightly larger than diameter of baking dish. Lay dough over top, sealing and crimping edges to rim of dish. Brush with beaten egg. Cut decorative designs (leaves, flower petals or geometric shapes) from leftover dough and arrange on crust. Brush again with egg. Cut several slits in crust to vent steam. Bake 1 to 1¼ hours, or until sauce is bubbling and crust is browned and crisp. (If crust browns too quickly, cover lightly with foil.) Serve hot.

Chinese Tea Bag Smoked Chicken

Chicken can be prepared ahead, wrapped in foil and frozen.

4 to 6 main-course or 10 buffet servings

1 tablespoon whole peppercorns
2 to 3 tablespoons salt (mixture should be salty)
1 4-pound chicken

1 tablespoon fragrant tea leaves or contents of 2 tea bags
1 tablespoon uncooked rice
1 tablespoon brown rice

Combine peppercorns and salt in small skillet and sauté until fragrant. Cool. Rub over skin and in cavity of chicken. Wrap chicken in foil; refrigerate overnight.

Wipe off peppercorn mixture. Pour about 2 inches water into wok or steamer. Place chicken on rack and set over water. Cover tightly and steam 45 minutes. Drain chicken well. Let stand at room temperature until cool and dry (this is very important in order for the chicken to smoke and brown properly).

To smoke: Line bottom of large pot (that has tight-fitting lid) with heavy-duty foil. Combine tea, rice and brown sugar and spread over foil. Set small rack in pot and place chicken on top, breast side up. Cover tightly (so smoke does not escape) and place over medium heat until you can hear leaves crackling. Let smoke 5 minutes. Turn off heat and let stand 5 minutes. Remove lid. If chicken is not nicely browned, cover again and let smoke over medium heat another 3 to 4 minutes. Slice chicken into bite-size pieces for buffet or cut into 4 to 6 servings if using as main course.

Glazed Cornish Hens

Cornish hens can be prepared a day or two in advance and refrigerated. When you know your schedule will be busy, it's not a bad idea to roast an extra bird or two to tuck in the refrigerator for later in the week. Chilled and wrapped in foil, the hens are well suited for a picnic.

2 servings

2 Cornish game hens (about 1 pound each)

For each bird:
1 garlic clove, minced
1 teaspoon dried thyme
¼ teaspoon salt

¼ teaspoon freshly ground pepper
½ cup (1 stick) butter
2 tablespoons fresh lemon juice
¼ teaspoon paprika
    Pinch of dried thyme

Preheat oven to 400°F. Rinse hens and pat dry with paper towels. Sprinkle cavities with garlic, thyme, salt and pepper. Tie legs together, bend wings back and truss with kitchen twine.

Melt ¼ cup butter in large skillet over medium-high heat and brown the hens on all sides. Transfer to shallow baking pan. Melt remaining butter in small pan. Add lemon juice, paprika and thyme. Brush birds generously. Roast until crisp and browned, about 40 minutes, brushing frequently with remaining butter mixture and drippings.

 Pork

Braised Pork with Caramelized Onion

A great do-ahead dish for company. The pork is marinated three days ahead and can be cooked up to one day before serving. Caramelized onion can also be made up to one day in advance.

8 to 10 servings

3 cups buttermilk
20 white peppercorns, bruised
4 juniper berries, lightly crushed
1 large garlic clove, crushed
1 bay leaf, broken up
1 4½- to 5-pound boned Boston butt or sirloin roast

3 tablespoons clarified butter
2 large onions, thinly sliced
    Pinch of sugar
¼ teaspoon salt

4 tablespoons clarified butter
1½ cups chicken stock
¼ cup (or more) Spanish Sherry wine vinegar
4 whole garlic cloves

2 to 3 tablespoons whipping cream
    Salt and freshly ground pepper
½ cup salted pine nuts
¼ cup raisins

Combine first 5 ingredients in large, deep nonaluminum bowl. Add pork, covering completely with marinade. Refrigerate 2 to 3 days, turning daily.

Heat 3 tablespoons butter in large skillet over medium-low heat. Add onion, cover and cook until soft and transparent, about 15 minutes. Increase heat to high, sprinkle onion with sugar and continue cooking, stirring constantly, until golden, about 5 minutes. Remove from heat and sprinkle with salt *(onion can be prepared up to 1 day ahead)*.

Remove pork from marinade; rinse gently under cold water and pat dry with paper towels. Heat remaining clarified butter in heavy 4- to 5-quart nonaluminum saucepan over medium-high heat. Add pork and brown well on all sides, about 15 to 20 minutes. Remove pork and pour off all fat in pan. Add stock to pan, scraping up any browned bits clinging to bottom. Return pork to pan with onion, ¼ cup vinegar and garlic and bring to gentle simmer. Cover and cook until pork is tender and meat thermometer inserted in thickest part registers 165°F, about 1½ to 2 hours. *(Can be prepared up to 1 day ahead to this point and reheated.)*

Transfer pork to cutting board and slice thinly. Cover and keep warm. Skim any fat from pan juices. Stir in cream (onion should be just moist; if sauce is too thin, reduce over high heat). Taste and adjust seasoning with salt, pepper and Sherry vinegar (onion should be tart-sweet). Arrange pork slices on heated platter and dollop with some of onion mixture. Spread remaining mixture around edge of platter. Sprinkle pork with nuts and raisins and serve.

Goulash with Wine-Braised Sauerkraut

This Hungarian stew can be prepared ahead and reheated before serving. It goes well with boiled potatoes dusted with fresh dill, a salad of romaine with thin slices of sweet red onion and a loaf of warm black bread.

8 servings

2 pounds sauerkraut (fresh, canned or packaged)

2 tablespoons vegetable oil
2 onions, chopped
3 to 4 tablespoons Hungarian sweet paprika
2 garlic cloves, minced
1 cup dry white wine
3½ pounds boneless pork stew meat, cut into 1-inch cubes

1½ teaspoons caraway seed
¼ cup tomato puree
2 cups chicken broth

½ cup whipping cream
½ cup sour cream
2 tablespoons all purpose flour
Salt and freshly ground pepper
Minced fresh parsley (optional garnish)

Thoroughly rinse sauerkraut under cold running water and drain well. Transfer to large bowl. Cover with cold water and let stand 20 minutes, changing water once. Squeeze sauerkraut to remove as much water as possible and set aside.

Heat oil in Dutch oven or large flameproof casserole over medium heat. Add onion and paprika and cook, stirring occasionally, until onion is limp and pale gold, about 10 minutes. Add garlic and cook 1 to 2 more minutes. Stir in ½ cup wine and bring mixture to boil. Add pork. Place sauerkraut over pork. Sprinkle caraway seed over top. Combine tomato puree and remaining wine in small bowl and whisk well. Stir tomato mixture and broth into pot. Bring mixture to boil. Reduce heat, cover and simmer, stirring occasionally and adding more liquid if necessary, 1 to 1½ hours.

Remove pork and sauerkraut from pot and keep warm. Combine cream, sour cream and flour in small bowl, blending well. Whisk cream mixture into sauce and cook over low heat, stirring constantly, 10 minutes. Return pork and sauerkraut to pot, blending well. Season with salt and pepper to taste. Ladle goulash into shallow bowls or rimmed plates. Sprinkle with parsley if desired and serve.

Mexican Pinto Beans and Pork with Avocado

This recipe is at its best when prepared two or three days in advance and reheated. Use to fill hot flour tortillas and serve with beer.

10 to 12 servings

1 pound dry pinto beans, soaked overnight in cold water

2 large fresh green chilies, seeded, deveined and chopped
1 large dried red chili, broken into small pieces
2 garlic cloves
1 tomato, peeled, seeded and chopped
½ cup water

4 tablespoons lard
1½ pounds lean boneless pork cut into 1-inch cubes

4 large onions, chopped

1½ teaspoons ground cumin
1 teaspoon ground coriander
1 teaspoon dried oregano or 1 tablespoon minced fresh oregano
3 to 5 cups beef broth
Salt and freshly ground pepper

2 firm-ripe avocados, peeled, seeded and coarsely chopped
Juice of 1 lime
1½ cups shredded Monterey Jack cheese

Drain most of water from beans. Turn into heavy 4- to 6-quart stovetop casserole or Dutch oven.

Combine chilies, garlic, tomato and water in processor or blender and mix until smooth. Set aside.

Heat lard in large heavy skillet over medium-high heat. Add about ⅓ of pork (do not crowd) and brown quickly. Remove with slotted spoon and add to beans. Repeat with remaining pork.

Add onion to skillet and brown quickly. Add chili puree, cumin, coriander and oregano and boil 2 minutes, scraping up any browned bits that cling to pan. Add to beans. Pour in enough broth to barely cover ingredients. Season with salt and pepper. Bring to gentle simmer, then cover partially and cook until pork and beans are tender, about 1½ to 2 hours.

Turn into large serving bowl. Garnish with avocado tossed with lime juice and sprinkle with shredded cheese.

If prepared ahead bring to room temperature and reheat in 350°F oven until bubbly. This recipe doubles and triples easily.

Homemade Italian Sausage

Sausage can be prepared ahead and frozen up to three months.

Makes about 16 sausages

2 pounds well-marbled pork butt, ground medium-fine (between 25 and 30 percent fat)
⅔ cup freshly grated imported Parmesan cheese
½ cup (well packed) minced fresh Italian parsley
¼ cup dry white wine
1 to 2 large garlic cloves, minced

1 tablespoon dried basil, crumbled
½ to 1 teaspoon minced hot red pepper
½ teaspoon salt
½ teaspoon dried oregano leaves, crumbled
¼ teaspoon freshly ground pepper
Narrow sausage casings, well rinsed

Combine all ingredients in large bowl and blend well, keeping mixture as light as possible. Using sausage stuffer, fill casings, twisting off 8-inch links as you work. Refrigerate immediately. Use within 1 day or freeze up to 3 months.

Sausage mixture can also be formed into patties or rolled into links.

Braised Country-Style Ribs with Wine, Kraut and Calvados

Ribs can be prepared up to two days ahead and reheated slowly over low heat.

4 to 6 servings

3 tablespoons oil
3 pounds country-style ribs cured 2 days in White Wine Brine (see following recipe), trimmed, rinsed and dried
1 large onion, chopped
1½ pounds sauerkraut, *well rinsed* and drained

¼ cup Calvados
1 cup dry white wine (preferably Alsatian Sylvaner)
½ cup unsalted beef stock
3 juniper berries, lightly crushed
Freshly ground pepper

Heat oil in heavy 5-quart saucepan over medium-high heat. Add ribs in batches and brown well on all sides; set aside. Add onion to saucepan and brown lightly. Stir in sauerkraut and Calvados and cook 2 minutes, stirring constantly. Add wine, stock and juniper berries and blend well. Reduce heat so mixture simmers. Bury ribs in mixture; cover and simmer until meat is tender, skimming fat as necessary, about 1 to 1½ hours. *(If mixture seems too thin, remove ribs and reduce liquid over high heat until sauerkraut is just barely moist.)* Season to taste with pepper. Arrange sauerkraut on platter and top with ribs.

White Wine Brine

1 quart water
⅔ cup salt
5 tablespoons firmly packed brown sugar
3 whole cloves
1 bay leaf
1 heaping teaspoon saltpeter (optional)
½ heaping teaspoon juniper berries
½ heaping teaspoon whole allspice

½ heaping teaspoon white peppercorns
½ heaping teaspoon dried thyme leaves, crumbled
¼ teaspoon whole yellow mustard seeds

3 pounds country-style spareribs
1 quart (4 cups) dry white wine

Combine all ingredients except wine and meat in 4-quart nonaluminum saucepan and bring to boil over medium heat. Increase heat to high, cover partially and let boil 3 minutes. Remove from heat and skim off any foam that has accumulated on surface. Let cool completely to room temperature.

Strain brine through cheesecloth into 5-quart pottery or stainless steel crock. Add ribs and wine. Weight with plate to keep meat submerged in brine. Let stand in cool place 2 days to cure.

Southern Maryland Stuffed Ham

This ham can be prepared one to two days in advance and refrigerated.

If ham is purchased enclosed in burlap bag, use bag instead of cheesecloth when wrapping stuffing around ham.

10 to 12 servings plus leftovers

3 pounds kale (thickest stems discarded), chopped
1 pound green onion, chopped
1 pound field cress (if available) or watercress, chopped
2 medium heads cabbage, cored and chopped
3 to 4 tablespoons whole mustard seed

2 tablespoons celery seed
3 tablespoons plus 1 teaspoon ground red pepper (or more to taste)
1 tablespoon plus 1 teaspoon salt

1 12- to 15-pound corned ham*

Combine kale, onion, field cress, cabbage, mustard seed, celery seed, red pepper and salt in large bowl.

Remove all skin from ham except near hock. Trim all but ½-inch layer of fat from ham. Pierce ham using long, slender, sharp knife, driving knife straight down and stopping 1 inch from bottom. Repeat, spacing staggered rows of slits 1 to 1½ inches apart, until entire ham is covered with slits.

Fill each slit with vegetable mixture until stuffing can be seen at top. Spread layer of stuffing on piece of cheesecloth large enough to surround ham. Set ham on cheesecloth. Pat remaining stuffing over top of ham. Bring cheesecloth up and around ham, distributing stuffing evenly, and secure with strong twine. Transfer ham to large pot. Add enough hot water to cover. Place over medium-high heat and bring to boil. Reduce heat, cover and simmer about 15 minutes per pound. Remove lid and let ham cool to room temperature in liquid. *(If prepared ahead and refrigerated, remove from refrigerator about 1½ hours before serving.)* To serve, cut ham into thin slices vertically across grain to expose stuffing.

*Fresh ham can be substituted for corned.

Jambon Chaud-Froid

Jambon Chaud-Froid can be prepared up to two days before serving.

20 to 30 servings

1 9- to 12-pound cooked ham, bone in, fat and rind removed

2 envelopes unflavored gelatin
⅔ cup chicken or beef stock
2 tablespoons vinegar
2 cups mayonnaise

¼ cup cold water

2 hard-cooked eggs, whites only (decoration)
2 large green onions, tops only (decoration)
   Boiling water

Make straight cut to bone 4 to 5 inches from shank. Make one cut at a 45° angle about 3 inches from end of ham to meet the bottom of first cut. *This slant cut acts as a "wedge" to hold the remaining slices in place.* Remove the wedge and set aside. Slice remaining ham thinly and evenly, cutting to the bone. Using a sawing motion, cut horizontally along leg bone to release slices. Return ham to its original shape, gently patting back any slices that may have slipped. Replace wedge to hold slices in place. Then transfer ham to baking sheet and refrigerate.

Measure ½ teaspoon gelatin and set aside. Combine stock and vinegar with remaining gelatin in small saucepan. Place over low heat and stir constantly until gelatin is dissolved. Remove from heat and set aside. When completely cooled, beat mixture into mayonnaise until smooth. Strain into bowl.

Spoon ⅓ mayonnaise mixture over ham. Chill until set. Coat evenly with half remaining mixture. Chill until set. When set, spoon remaining mixture over ham to finish coating. Chill.

Just before ready to decorate, sprinkle reserved ½ teaspoon gelatin over cold water in small saucepan or heatproof dish (a metal 1-cup measure is ideal). Place over low heat and stir constantly until gelatin is completely dissolved. Remove from heat and set aside to cool and thicken slightly.

To decorate, cut "petals" from hard-cooked egg whites and "stems" and "leaves" from green onion tops. Dip briefly into boiling water, then into cooled clear gelatin. Set in place. Transfer to platter and refrigerate at least 2 hours.

To serve, cut through chaud-froid and remove wedge slice. Continue cutting through chaud-froid to lift off each slice separately.

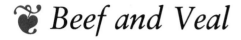 Beef and Veal

Braised Beef Birds with Olives and Capers

Beef Birds can be prepared ahead and refrigerated in sauce for several days.

To highlight its piquant Southern Italian flavors, serve this dish with pasta or rice, a young, rough, full-bodied red wine such as a Grumello or Bardolino and baskets of coarse country bread.

4 to 6 servings

Stuffing
5 thick slices spicy Italian salami, minced
3 ounces mortadella, minced
5 ounces Italian Parmesan cheese, grated
3 green onions, minced
⅓ cup minced parsley (preferably Italian)
1 small garlic clove, minced
1 egg yolk
½ teaspoon dried basil or 1½ teaspoons fresh
   Salt and freshly ground pepper

Beef Birds
1½ to 1¾ pounds beef top round, well trimmed and cut into 4 slices ¼ inch thick
8 thin slices pancetta (Italian dry-cured unsmoked bacon)*

Braising Sauce
5 tablespoons full-bodied olive oil
2 medium onions, minced
10 large garlic cloves, lightly crushed
¼ cup minced parsley
1 tablespoon dried basil or 3 tablespoons minced fresh
¾ teaspoon dried oregano or 2½ teaspoons minced fresh
¼ cup full-bodied red wine (Barolo, Grumello or Bardolino)
2 generous teaspoons anchovy paste
1 1-pound 12-ounce can plum tomatoes
15 oil-cured black olives, pitted and chopped

   Juice and grated peel of 1 medium lemon
1 tablespoon drained capers
   Dash of hot pepper sauce (optional)
   Salt and freshly ground pepper

For stuffing: Combine all ingredients in large bowl. Cover and chill for 1 to 2 hours, or up to 2 days.

For beef birds: Pound beef slices between 2 sheets of waxed paper until very thin but not torn. Cut beef slices in half and top each with slice of pancetta. Spread stuffing over meat, leaving ½-inch border on all sides. Starting at narrow end, roll up each slice, tucking in edges as you roll to prevent stuffing from leaking out during cooking. Tie with string to form compact cylinders.

For sauce: Heat oil in large skillet over medium-high heat. Add beef birds and brown well on all sides. (Do not let pieces touch during browning.) Transfer birds to platter using slotted spoon. Add onion and sauté quickly until browned. Stir in garlic and cook, stirring often, until it just begins to color. Add parsley and cook another few seconds. Stir in herbs and wine. Bring to boil and cook until wine is reduced by half. Add anchovy paste and tomatoes and stir until blended. Add beef birds and turn to coat well with sauce. Reduce heat, cover and simmer until beef is barely tender, about 1 hour. Stir in olives and continue cooking until beef is tender when pierced with fork. Skim off any fat accumulated on surface. *(Beef birds may be prepared ahead to this point and refrigerated several days.)*

Just before serving, discard strings on beef birds; reheat gently if necessary. Stir in lemon juice and peel, capers, hot pepper sauce and salt and pepper.

*Prosciutto can be substituted.

Dijon and Cognac Beef Stew

*This country-style dish is
even better the second day.
The basic stew can be prepared two to three days
ahead and refrigerated, or
frozen up to three months.*

4 to 6 servings

4 ounces salt pork, blanched 5
minutes (rind removed and
reserved), cut into small dice
1 large onion, chopped
3 large shallots, chopped
2 pounds lean beef chuck, trimmed
and cut into 1-inch cubes
All purpose flour
Butter

¼ cup good quality Cognac
2 cups beef stock
1 tablespoon Dijon mustard

1 tablespoon coarse-ground French
mustard
2 large carrots, cut into bite-size
pieces
Salt and freshly ground pepper

2 tablespoons butter
7 ounces small fresh mushrooms,
halved
¼ cup full-bodied red wine
1 tablespoon coarse-ground French
mustard

Cook salt pork in heavy, large, nonaluminum skillet over medium heat until
golden. Remove with slotted spoon and transfer to 4-quart saucepan or Dutch
oven. Add onion and shallot to skillet and brown quickly over high heat. Transfer
to saucepan using slotted spoon. Coat beef cubes with flour, shaking off excess.
Add butter to same skillet if necessary and melt over medium heat. Add meat in
three batches and brown well on all sides. (Do not allow cubes to touch, or they
will steam rather than brown.) Adjust heat as necessary so that particles in pan
do not burn. Transfer meat to saucepan.

Pour Cognac into hot skillet and cook until only a thin glaze of liquid remains.
Stir in stock and bring to boil, scraping up any browned bits clinging to pan. Add
to beef along with Dijon mustard, 1 tablespoon coarse-ground mustard and reserved
pork rind. Bring to simmer, cover partially and cook until beef is barely tender,
about 2 to 3 hours. Add carrot and cook until fork tender. Season to taste with
salt and pepper. *(Stew can be prepared up to this point and stored in refrigerator
two to three days, or in freezer up to three months.)*

Just before serving, bring stew to simmer. Heat remaining butter in medium
skillet over medium-high heat. Add mushrooms and brown well. Add wine and
remaining mustard and boil about 20 seconds. Stir mixture into stew and let
simmer for 5 minutes.

Red Cooked Anise Beef

*Can be made ahead.
Accompany with rice, stir-
fried asparagus or broccoli
and cold beer.*

8 servings

2 tablespoons (or more) peanut oil
3½ pounds beef stew meat,
patted dry
1½ cups water
¼ cup soy sauce
3 tablespoons dry Sherry
2 tablespoons sugar
4 slices fresh ginger, minced (about
½ to 1 teaspoon)

3 garlic cloves, minced
2 star anise or 2 teaspoons Chinese
five-spice powder*
1 tablespoon cornstarch mixed with
½ tablespoon cold water
Diagonally sliced green onion
(garnish)

Heat 2 tablespoons oil in wok or Dutch oven over medium-high heat until very
hot. Add meat in 4 batches and brown all sides well, adding more oil after each
batch if necessary. Return all meat to wok. Stir in water, soy sauce, Sherry, sugar,

ginger, garlic and star anise. Bring mixture to boil. Reduce heat, cover and simmer until meat is tender, about 1½ to 2 hours, stirring occasionally. Remove meat from wok using slotted spoon. Skim fat from sauce. Thicken with cornstarch mixture as desired. Return meat to wok and blend well. Garnish each serving with sliced green onion.

*If star anise and Chinese five-spice powder are unavailable, improvise the seasoning by combining 1 teaspoon ground ginger with ¼ teaspoon each cinnamon, ground aniseed, ground allspice and ground cloves.

Ragoût de la Gironde

The flavor will be rich if stew is prepared several days ahead and then refrigerated to mellow.

Much of the charm of this dish is its flexibility. Almost any meat can go into it, and your own seasoning preferences will give it a stamp of individuality. The cooking method is unique: Half of the ingredients are arranged in the pot, cooked slowly in the oven, cooled and then refrigerated overnight. This first batch, rich with concentrated flavors, acts as a "starter" when the remaining ingredients are added the next day.

6 to 8 servings

½ pound bacon or salt pork slices	Salt and freshly ground pepper
8 thinly sliced carrots	2 pounds boneless pork, cut into 2-inch cubes
2 to 3 bay leaves (or to taste)	1 pound mushrooms, stemmed
1 small bunch parsley, chopped	
¼ cup snipped fresh thyme or 2 teaspoons dried thyme, crumbled	½ cup brandy
3 garlic cloves, minced	Dry red wine (about two 750-ml bottles)
8 fresh or dried figs, halved	
6 onions, sliced	
2 pounds beef stew meat, cut into 2-inch cubes	

Preheat oven to 325°F. Grease Dutch oven or large casserole. Arrange enough bacon or salt pork slices in bottom to cover. Layer with about half of carrots and 2 to 3 bay leaves. Add layer of chopped parsley, thyme and garlic. Arrange figs over seasonings and 2 sliced onions over figs. Top with half of beef and refrigerate remainder. Add another layer of 2 sliced onions. Sprinkle with salt and pepper. Top with half of pork and refrigerate remainder. Arrange half of mushrooms over and sprinkle lightly with salt and pepper.

Warm brandy in small saucepan. Ignite and pour over ragoût, shaking pan gently until flame subsides. Add enough red wine to cover all ingredients. Cover and bake until wine is reduced by half, about 2 to 3 hours, adjusting oven temperature as necessary so ragoût is just bubbling slightly. Set aside to cool. Refrigerate mixture overnight.

Bring ragoût back to room temperature. Preheat oven to 325°F. Season remaining beef and pork with salt and pepper. Layer remaining carrots, beef, onion, pork and mushrooms over top of ragoût. Pour in enough wine to barely cover all ingredients. Cover and bake until wine is reduced by half (ragoût should be bubbling slightly). Ladle ragoût into bowls and serve.

Half of stew can be reserved to use as base for next Ragoût de la Gironde. Fill pot with layers of same ingredients (or substitute ham, lamb, sausage, chicken or turkey for beef and pork). Add enough wine just to cover all ingredients. Cover and cook until wine is reduced by half. Remember that new ingredients are on top and concentrated sauce is at bottom, so be sure to include some rich sauce from bottom with each serving.

Stufato (Beef in Red Wine)

This dish can be prepared ahead and frozen.

2 servings

1 pound beef chuck, cut into 1-inch cubes
2 tablespoons olive oil
1 onion, sliced
1 cup dry red wine
½ cup canned Italian plum tomatoes

3 garlic cloves, minced
1 tablespoon minced fresh parsley
1 bay leaf
½ teaspoon dried basil, crumbled
¼ teaspoon dried thyme, crumbled
Salt and freshly ground pepper

Pat meat dry with paper towels. Heat oil in heavy saucepan over medium-high heat. Add meat and brown on all sides. Add onion and sauté until limp. Stir in ½ cup wine. Add tomatoes, garlic, parsley, bay leaf, basil and thyme. Reduce heat, cover and simmer 1 hour. Add remaining wine and continue simmering for another hour. Discard bay leaf. Season with salt and pepper and serve.

New Mexico Chili with Tamale-Cheese Topping

This chili can be prepared several days ahead and refrigerated, or frozen up to three months. Reheat and enhance with Tamale-Cheese Topping.

New Mexico chili is quite different from Tex-Mex and Mexican renditions, using a salsa blended from dried red chilies and herbs, browned diced meat and little or no tomato. Serve this with a frosted glass of foamy dark beer.

6 to 8 servings

Salsa
20 dried red Las Cruces chilies or large green chilies

3 cups beef broth
2 large garlic cloves
2 tablespoons dried basil
1½ tablespoons dried oregano
1 to 1½ tablespoons whole cumin seed
½ teaspoon whole coriander seed
½ teaspoon sugar

Chili
¼ cup lard or vegetable oil

3½ to 4 pounds beef bottom round or rump, cut into very small dice
4 medium onions, chopped
3 tablespoons tomato paste (optional)
1 cup (about) beef stock

Tamale-Cheese Topping (see following recipe)

Salt and freshly ground pepper
Hot chili powder or ground red pepper (optional)
Pinch of sugar (optional)
Vinegar (optional)

For salsa: Preheat oven to 200°F. Spread chilies on baking sheet and roast 8 minutes. Let cool, then hold under running water to remove seeds, veins and any bruised areas.

Combine broth, garlic, basil, oregano, cumin, coriander, sugar and chilies in blender and puree until smooth. Set aside. (*Can be prepared ahead and refrigerated for several days.*)

For chili: Heat lard or oil in large skillet over medium-high heat. Add beef in batches and cook until well browned. Transfer to 4-quart saucepan or Dutch oven using slotted spoon. Add onion to skillet and cook until browned. Stir in tomato paste and salsa and bring to simmer, scraping up any browned bits clinging to bottom of pan. Turn mixture into saucepan and add stock. Cover partially and simmer until beef is tender, 2 to 3 hours. Add more stock if mixture seems dry.

Preheat oven to 375°F.

Taste chili and adjust seasoning. If too mild, add chili powder or ground red pepper. If too hot, add sugar and about 1 tablespoon vinegar. Skim fat from surface. Transfer chili to 2- to 3-quart soufflé dish or deep casserole. (*Chili can be prepared several days ahead to this point and refrigerated, or frozen for up to 3 months.*)

Cover and bake until chili is hot and bubbly in center. Remove from oven and spread Tamale-Cheese Topping over top. Return to oven and bake until golden brown, about 45 minutes to 1 hour. Serve immediately.

Tamale-Cheese Topping

¾ cup water
¼ teaspoon salt
¼ cup plus 2 tablespoons prepared tortilla flour or yellow cornmeal

½ cup sour cream
2 egg yolks

4 ounces Monterey Jack cheese or queso blanco, shredded
Salt and freshly ground pepper

Combine water and salt in 1½-quart saucepan and bring to boil over high heat. Reduce heat and stir in tortilla flour or cornmeal. Cook, stirring constantly, until smooth and thick, about 5 minutes. Let cool about 15 minutes.

Add sour cream, egg yolks and cheese and beat until well blended. Taste and adjust seasoning. Spread over hot chili.

Whole Stuffed Cabbage Alsatian

Can be prepared up to three days ahead, covered and refrigerated, or frozen for several months.

The cabbage leaves are reassembled with layers of a savory meat filling, or the filling can be rolled in individual leaves. Serve with baked potatoes, homemade applesauce and a magnum of Champagne.

6 to 8 servings

1 large head green cabbage

Filling
2 heaping teaspoons sour salt or citric acid (available at most markets or drug stores)
½ cup cold water
3 eggs
1 large onion
3 pounds lean ground beef
¼ cup *uncooked* long-grain white rice
¼ cup red wine
2 to 3 teaspoons salt
¾ to 1 teaspoon freshly ground white pepper

Sauce
1 29-ounce can sauerkraut, undrained

1 16-ounce can tomatoes, undrained
1 10¾-ounce can tomato soup
1 cup dark brown sugar, firmly packed
1 cup golden raisins
½ cup red wine
2 large carrots, thinly sliced on the diagonal

1 24-inch square of cheesecloth
String

10 to 12 gingersnaps, crushed

To prepare cabbage: Make cuts around cabbage stem with paring knife. Steam stem side down in colander over 2 to 3 inches boiling water 10 to 12 minutes, or until leaves are pliable and will not break when rolled. Drain and separate leaves. Scrape heavy vein from each leaf to make it lie flat.

For filling: Dissolve sour salt in water in small bowl. Puree eggs with onion in food processor or blender. Combine beef, rice, wine, salt and pepper with 2 to 3 tablespoons dissolved sour salt and onion-egg puree in large bowl and blend well. *The filling should be strongly seasoned and tart to the taste, or its flavor will be flat compared to that of the sauce.*

For sauce: Combine sauerkraut, tomatoes, soup, sugar, raisins, wine and carrot in large bowl and mix well.

To assemble: Spread out cheesecloth square. Place 6 to 7 cabbage leaves in slightly overlapping circle with stem ends facing outer edge of circle. Cover center with large cabbage leaf. Spoon half of filling into centers of leaves, gently spreading toward outer edges but leaving about 2-inch border of cabbage leaves. Cover with second smaller layer of leaves and spread with ⅔ of remaining filling. Make third layer of leaves and cover with remaining filling. Hold 2 corners of cheesecloth with each hand and bring edges together to reshape leaves into form of whole cabbage. Tie securely with string and cut off any excess cheesecloth above string.

Break any remaining cabbage pieces into bottom of 6- to 8-quart Dutch oven. Place cheesecloth-covered cabbage, rounded side up and tied side down, in pot and cover with sauce. Bring to simmer over medium heat, reduce heat to low, cover and cook 1½ hours, basting occasionally. Remove cabbage and place rounded side up in ovenproof serving dish. Remove cheesecloth. Cut cabbage into 8 wedges.

Preheat oven to 350°F. Discard cabbage pieces from bottom of Dutch oven. Add crushed gingersnaps to remaining sauce. Cook over medium heat until gingersnaps are dissolved and sauce is thickened. Taste and adjust seasonings. *(Flavor should be sweet and sour, so add more salt, pepper, gingersnaps or lemon juice in combination to enhance taste.)* Spread sauce evenly over and between wedges. Cover with foil "tent" and bake 20 minutes. Remove foil and bake an additional 25 minutes, basting once or twice during baking. Baste again just before serving.

Note: For individual cabbage rolls, place heaping tablespoon of filling (depending on size of leaf) on stem end of each leaf, fold in sides and roll. Place seam side down in Dutch oven with extra cabbage if desired. Cover with sauce and cook as directed for whole cabbage. Use leftover sauce with tiny meatballs.

Moussaka (Greek Eggplant-Meat Casserole)

Casserole can be refrigerated or frozen before custard is added. Bring to room temperature before baking.

6 to 8 servings

3 or 4 eggplants, peeled and cut into slices ⅜ inch thick
Salted water
Flour

½ cup (about) peanut oil

2 tablespoons olive oil
1 large onion, diced (1 cup)
2 tomatoes, peeled and diced or 2 cups canned plum tomatoes, drained
1½ pounds lean ground beef
1 teaspoon salt
Freshly ground pepper

Custard Topping
¼ cup (½ stick) butter
5 tablespoons flour
½ cup whipping cream
1 cup water
½ teaspoon salt
Freshly ground pepper
Dash of nutmeg

1 cup (about) freshly grated Parmesan cheese

2 eggs
2 teaspoons fresh lemon juice

Soak eggplant slices in salted water 20 minutes. Drain, then blot on paper towels. Coat with flour.

Preheat oven to 450°F. Grease 8 × 15-inch casserole and cover rimmed baking sheet with heavy-duty foil. Coat foil with about ½ cup peanut oil. Add eggplant, turning to coat well. Bake about 20 minutes. Turn off oven and let eggplant stand another 30 minutes.

Heat olive oil in large skillet. Add onion and sauté 1 minute. Add tomatoes and cook another minute. Add beef and cook through. Season to taste with salt and pepper. Drain meat and pour drippings over eggplant. Let meat cool while making custard.

Melt butter in medium skillet. Stir in flour and cook 1 minute. Add cream, water, salt, pepper and nutmeg and cook until very thick, about 10 to 12 minutes, stirring frequently. Remove from heat, cover and set aside.

Preheat oven to 350°F. Layer eggplant and meat mixture to within 1 inch of top of casserole, sprinkling each layer with some of cheese. Bake 15 minutes.

Beat eggs and whisk into cooled cream sauce. Add lemon juice. Taste and adjust seasoning. Spoon over casserole. Continue baking on lowest shelf of oven until hot, browned and puffed, about 35 minutes. Cut into squares.

Ragoût (German)

This casserole-style ragoût can be made ahead and refrigerated or frozen until serving day.

4 servings

¼ pound cooked smoked tongue
1 whole chicken breast, boned and skinned
½ pound veal

¼ cup (½ stick) butter
2 shallots, minced
½ pound mushrooms, sliced
¼ cup flour
½ cup chicken stock
¾ cup whipping cream
½ cup Mosel or white wine

1 teaspoon sugar
1 teaspoon coarse salt or ½ teaspoon regular salt
Freshly ground pepper

2 egg yolks
2 teaspoons fresh lemon juice
2 tablespoons breadcrumbs
2 tablespoons freshly grated Parmesan cheese

Freshly cooked egg noodles

Cut tongue into julienne strips about ¼ inch thick and 2 inches long. Remove fillets from chicken and strip out tough tendons. Cut fillets in half diagonally. Cut rest of meat with the grain into pieces same size as fillets. Remove any skin and tough parts from veal. Cut meat into pieces same size as chicken.

Melt butter in large skillet. Add shallot and mushrooms and stir-cook 2 minutes. Add chicken and veal and stir-cook until meats turn white. Stir in flour. Add stock, ½ cup cream, wine, sugar, salt and pepper and stir-cook until thickened. Simmer about 5 minutes. Add tongue and mix well.

Beat together remaining ¼ cup cream, yolks and lemon juice. Remove skillet from heat and stir in yolk mixture. Turn into shallow baking dish. Combine crumbs and cheese and sprinkle over casserole. *(Casserole can be refrigerated or frozen at this point. Bring to room temperature before completing preparation.)*

Preheat broiler. Place casserole about 4 inches from heat source until browned. Serve over bed of egg noodles.

Veal and Sorrel Stew in Gougère Ring

Stew can be made ahead and refrigerated. Reheat before serving in Gougère Ring.

6 to 8 servings

2 cups Gewürztraminer or dry white wine
2 cups water
1 onion, stuck with 2 cloves
1 bouquet garni (sliced leek, parsley, thyme, bay leaf and garlic clove)
1½ pounds veal stew meat, cut into 1-inch cubes
1½ pounds boneless pork, cut into 1-inch cubes

1 tablespoon butter

¼ pound sorrel, rinsed and stemmed

3 tablespoons butter
3 tablespoons all purpose flour

½ cup whipping cream
2 egg yolks
Salt and freshly ground pepper
Gougère Ring (see following recipe)
Fresh sorrel chiffonade (optional garnish)

Combine wine, water, onion and bouquet garni in Dutch oven or large casserole and bring to boil over medium-high heat. Reduce heat and add veal and pork. Cover and simmer mixture very gently until veal and pork are tender when pierced, about 1½ hours.

Melt 1 tablespoon butter in small skillet. Add sorrel and cook over low heat until very soft. Puree with back of spoon. Set aside to cool.

Remove meat from broth using slotted spoon. Discard bouquet garni. Melt 3 tablespoons butter in large saucepan over low heat. Stir in flour and cook until roux is pale gold. Add broth and bring to boil. Reduce heat to low and simmer until slightly thickened, about 20 minutes, stirring occasionally.

Combine cream and egg yolks in large bowl and whisk thoroughly. Stir about ¼ cup warm sauce into cream mixture. Slowly pour cream mixture into sauce, whisking well. Return meat to sauce and simmer gently until heated through. Stir in reserved sorrel puree, blending well. Season stew with salt and pepper to taste. Spoon stew into center of Gougère Ring. Garnish with sorrel chiffonade if desired.

Gougère Ring

6 to 8 servings

1 cup water	4 to 5 eggs
½ cup (1 stick) butter, cut into ½-inch pieces	¾ cup diced Gruyère cheese
1 cup all purpose flour, sifted Pinch of salt	1 egg yolk beaten with 1 tablespoon water

Preheat oven to 425°F. Combine water and butter in large saucepan and bring to rapid boil over high heat. Remove from heat. Immediately stir in flour and salt. Place over medium heat and beat vigorously until dough pulls away from sides of pan and films bottom. Cool mixture for 5 minutes. Add eggs one at a time, beating well after each addition, until mixture is glossy and smooth. Stir in cheese, blending well.

Dampen baking sheet with cold water, shaking off excess (this will help pastry rise). Arrange large spoonfuls of dough next to each other in wreath pattern on sheet. Brush top with egg yolk mixture, being careful not to drip it on side. Bake 15 minutes. Reduce oven temperature to 375°F and bake until puffed and brown, about 15 more minutes. Slit gougère several places on side and return to turned-off oven with door ajar for 15 minutes to dry. Serve hot or at room temperature.

 # Lamb

Ragoût of Lamb à la Grecque

Ragoût can be prepared up to three days ahead and reheated. It also freezes well.

Four cups cooked rice pilaf tossed with 1 cup finely minced fresh parsley and 2 tablespoons finely minced fresh mint goes well with this flavorful dish.

6 to 8 servings

1 large eggplant, peeled and cut into 1-inch cubes Salt	1 large sprig fresh oregano (preferably Greek with flowers)
6 to 8 tablespoons olive oil	1 bay leaf
1 tablespoon butter	1 teaspoon cumin
3 pounds lean boned shoulder of lamb, cubed and patted dry Salt and freshly ground pepper Flour Pinch of sugar	2 cups lamb stock or beef bouillon
	1 tablespoon arrowroot dissolved in small amount of lamb stock or beef bouillon
2 cups finely minced onion	2 tablespoons finely minced fresh oregano
3 garlic cloves, finely minced	2 garlic cloves, crushed
1 28-ounce can Italian plum tomatoes, thoroughly drained and chopped	½ cup Greek black olives, pitted and halved (optional) Finely minced fresh parsley (garnish)
1 tablespoon tomato paste	

Arrange eggplant in single layer on double thickness of paper towels. Sprinkle with salt and let drain 1 hour. Rinse, dry thoroughly and set aside.

Position rack in center of oven and preheat to 350°F. Heat some of oil and butter in heavy 12-inch skillet over medium-high heat. Add lamb in batches and brown on all sides, removing with slotted spoon and adding oil and butter to skillet as necessary. Return all meat to skillet and season with salt and pepper. Sprinkle lightly with flour and sugar and sauté, shaking pan until lamb is nicely glazed, 2 to 3 minutes. Transfer to heatproof casserole using slotted spoon.

Add a little more oil and butter to skillet. Add onion and minced garlic and sauté until vegetables are soft and lightly browned, scraping up any browned bits clinging to bottom of skillet, about 2 to 3 minutes. Add next 5 ingredients and bring to boil. Pour over lamb. Blend in stock or bouillon. Cover and braise until lamb is just fork tender, about 1½ hours.

Meanwhile, heat more olive oil in heavy 10-inch skillet over medium-high heat. Add eggplant and sauté until nicely browned on all sides. Transfer to colander or paper towels to drain.

Remove lamb from baking dish using slotted spoon. Strain pan juices through fine sieve. Return to baking dish and place over high direct heat. Whisk in dissolved arrowroot, mixing constantly until sauce heavily coats spoon. Reduce heat and add oregano and crushed garlic. Return lamb to casserole. Add eggplant and olives and heat through. Season to taste with salt and pepper. Sprinkle with minced fresh parsley just before serving.

Spicy Malaysian Lamb

Stew can be prepared ahead and reheated at serving time.

Serve on a bed of fluffy white rice. A chilled fruity white wine such as Gewürztraminer can hold its own with this spicy dish, but cold lager is an even better accompaniment.

6 to 8 servings

2 tablespoons cider vinegar
2 tablespoons fresh lime juice
1½ teaspoons chili powder (or to taste)
3 pounds boneless lamb stew meat, trimmed of excess fat

3 tablespoons vegetable oil
2½ cups thinly sliced onion (about 2 medium)
1 4-ounce can chopped mild green chilies
1½ tablespoons minced fresh ginger

1½ teaspoons salt
½ teaspoon turmeric
2 garlic cloves, minced (about ½ teaspoon)
1 28-ounce can whole tomatoes, drained (reserve liquid) and chopped
¾ cup water
Salt and freshly ground pepper
Chopped fresh coriander (garnish)

Combine vinegar, lime juice and chili powder in medium bowl and blend well. Add lamb and marinate, turning frequently, about 15 minutes.

Heat oil in heavy large pot or Dutch oven over medium-high heat. Add lamb in batches, browning well on all sides. Remove meat from pot using slotted spoon. Reduce heat to low, add onion, chilies, ginger, salt, turmeric and garlic and cook, stirring frequently, until onion is limp and translucent, about 5 to 10 minutes. Blend in meat, tomatoes, reserved liquid and ¾ cup water. Bring to boil. Reduce heat, cover and simmer until lamb is tender and sauce is slightly thickened, about 1½ hours, stirring occasionally. Season with salt and pepper to taste. Ladle into soup bowls and sprinkle with chopped fresh coriander.

Kufta (Filled Meatballs)

Meatballs and broth can be made ahead and frozen separately. Boil meatballs after freezing.

Makes 12 to 18 meatballs

Filling
½ pound ground lamb
2 large onions, finely chopped
¼ green pepper, finely chopped
¼ cup minced fresh parsley
¼ teaspoon *each* salt, freshly ground pepper and paprika

Broth
Lamb bones
1 8-ounce can tomato sauce

Outer Layer
1 pound very lean lamb, ground twice
¼ to ½ pound very lean ground beef
1 cup very fine bulgur
1 egg
Dash of ground red pepper
Salt and freshly ground pepper

For filling: Sauté meat in large skillet until browned. Add onion and cook slowly 30 minutes. Add green pepper and parsley and cook 10 minutes longer. Stir in seasoning and cook 5 minutes. Chill until ready to use.

For broth: Boil lamb bones in salted water (broth need not be rich), removing scum as it accumulates. Stir in tomato sauce and blend well.

For outer layer: Combine all ingredients. (Keep small bowl of ice water handy and continue dipping hands as you mix. This helps blend ingredients, makes meat easier to mold and expands bulgur.) Knead like dough for about 15 minutes, dipping hands into ice water periodically until meat is sticky. Mold into balls about the size of an egg. Form indentation using thumb and forefinger (rotate ball in palm of hand as you press sides to form even cavity) to make wall as thin as possible, about ¼ to ½ inch. (Cavity should be about 1½ to 2 inches deep and 2½ inches wide.)

Place 1 tablespoon filling in each meatball; bring edges around and seal opening to make it as smooth as possible.

Add Kufta a few at a time to broth and boil until they float to surface and are cooked through, about 10 minutes. Serve with or without broth.

For a quicker broth, half-fill 6-quart casserole with water; add 1 can tomato soup and salt to taste and bring to boil.

Ingredients for outer layer also can be formed into balls about size of large olives and boiled in broth. Serve as soup course.

Shepherd's Pie with Tarragon

This can be assembled and refrigerated up to two days before baking.

4 to 6 servings

4 large baking potatoes, baked and cooled slightly
3 tablespoons butter
1 tablespoon minced green onion tops
¼ teaspoon dried tarragon
Salt and freshly ground pepper
1 egg yolk, beaten

2 tablespoons oil or bacon fat

1 large onion, chopped
1½ pounds lean lamb (from leg), cut into small cubes
3 to 6 tablespoons rich lamb or beef stock
¼ teaspoon Worcestershire sauce
⅛ teaspoon dried tarragon

Butter (optional)

Split potatoes in half and scoop pulp into bowl. Add butter, green onion, tarragon, salt and pepper and blend well. Cool to lukewarm, then whip in egg yolk thoroughly. Set aside.

Position rack in center of oven and preheat to 375°F. Butter deep 1½-quart baking dish. Heat oil or bacon fat in large skillet over medium-high heat. Add onion and sauté until softened. Increase heat to high, add lamb and sauté 2 minutes. Stir in stock, Worcestershire and tarragon. Remove from heat, taste and adjust seasoning.

Spread ⅔ of potato mixture over bottom and sides of prepared dish. Add lamb mixture with all juices. Spread remaining potatoes evenly over top, covering completely. Dot with butter if desired and bake about 1½ hours.

Potato skins can be frozen. Cut into small pieces and deep fry. They may be served as an appetizer.

 # Game

Polenta and Rabbit Pie Hunter's Style

This dish is best when assembled one or two days in advance.

A new approach to a Tuscan tradition. Our version layers the rich stew with polenta flavored with herbs and freshly grated Parmesan cheese. Although domestic rabbit, found fresh or frozen in many supermarkets, is used here, classically the recipe calls for wild hare, and if it is available in your area, do use it. Longer cooking time will be required to tenderize it, but the results will be richer and fuller. Chicken may be substituted for rabbit and produces a more delicate result. Serve with marinated tomatoes and fresh peppers, followed by fresh fruit for dessert. A Chianti Classico or Barolo is a good accompaniment.

6 to 8 servings

Rabbit
1 2½-pound (about) rabbit, cut into 8 pieces
Liver from rabbit
1 cup dry red wine
1 garlic clove, halved
½ teaspoon whole leaf rosemary
¼ teaspoon whole leaf marjoram
Pinch of whole leaf sage

Flour

6 tablespoons olive oil
1 large onion, chopped
1½ cups peeled, seeded fresh tomatoes or drained canned tomatoes
⅓ cup black olives (preferably Kalamata olives packed in olive oil and vinegar)
2 tablespoons dried wild mushrooms (preferably French or Italian variety), soaked in ½ cup hot water, undrained
1 teaspoon whole leaf basil
1 bay leaf
Salt and freshly ground pepper

Polenta
6½ cups water
2 cups coarse cornmeal
3 ounces (¾ cup) freshly grated imported Parmesan cheese
2 tablespoons (¼ stick) butter
1½ teaspoons whole leaf sage, crumbled
1 teaspoon salt

Butter (optional)

For rabbit: Combine rabbit, liver, wine, garlic, rosemary, marjoram and sage in large bowl. Cover and refrigerate 24 hours, turning occasionally.

Drain rabbit, reserving marinade and garlic halves; mince garlic and set aside. Pat rabbit dry with paper towels and dredge in flour, shaking off excess.

Heat oil in large skillet over medium-high heat. Brown rabbit very well in 2 batches (do not crowd, or rabbit will steam rather than brown). Transfer rabbit to platter. Add onion to skillet and sauté until golden. Add garlic and sauté another minute. Stir in reserved marinade and boil about 2 minutes, scraping up any browned bits clinging to bottom of skillet. Add tomatoes, olives, mushrooms with liquid, herbs, salt and pepper and blend well. Bring sauce to gentle simmer. Return rabbit to skillet, covering with sauce. Cover and simmer until rabbit is tender, about 1¼ hours.

Remove from heat, skim off fat and allow sauce to cool. Taste; if sauce seems weak, remove rabbit, return skillet to high heat and reduce sauce by ⅓. When rabbit is cool enough to handle, remove meat from bones and cut into bite-size chunks. Blend into sauce. (Pit olives at this point, if desired.)

For polenta: Generously grease 8-inch-square baking dish. Bring water to boil in 4-quart heavy-bottomed saucepan. Gradually stir in cornmeal, adding slowly so water does not stop boiling. Reduce heat to medium-low and cook, stirring constantly, about 20 minutes. Stir in remaining ingredients and blend well. Pour into prepared dish and cool. Cover and refrigerate overnight.

To assemble: Position rack in center of oven and preheat to 350°F. Generously butter 8- to 9-cup soufflé dish. Carefully turn polenta out of pan and slice thinly. Layer bottom of dish with ⅓ of polenta. Cover with ½ of rabbit. Add another ⅓ of polenta and remaining rabbit and top with remaining polenta. Dot top with butter if desired. Bake until hot throughout, about 1 to 1½ hours.

Rabbit Stew with Cognac and Mustard

Stew can be made ahead; reheat before serving.

Serve with thin egg noodles, a pungent watercress and endive salad and a medium-light wine such as a Beaujolais, Zinfandel or Côtes-du-Rhône.

8 servings

2 tablespoons (¼ stick) butter (or more)
2 tablespoons vegetable oil (or more)
2 large rabbits (about 3 pounds each) or 2 chickens, cut into serving pieces and patted dry
3 tablespoons Cognac
4 medium onions, quartered
2 garlic cloves, minced
2 tablespoons all purpose flour
1 teaspoon dried rosemary, crumbled
1 teaspoon dried oregano, crumbled

½ teaspoon dried tarragon, crumbled
½ teaspoon dried sage leaves, crumbled
2 cups dry white wine or chicken broth

1 cup whipping cream
2 tablespoons Dijon mustard
Salt and freshly ground pepper
¼ cup minced fresh parsley (garnish)

Preheat oven to 350°F. Heat 2 tablespoons butter and 2 tablespoons oil in heavy Dutch oven or large casserole. Add rabbit and brown on all sides. Pour Cognac in corner of pan and ignite, spooning Cognac over rabbit until flames subside. Remove meat from pot using slotted spoon. Add onion and garlic to pot and sauté until limp and golden, about 10 minutes, adding more oil and butter if necessary. Stir in flour and cook until flour just begins to brown, about 1 to 2 minutes. Add rosemary, oregano, tarragon, sage and wine and blend well. Return rabbit to pot. Bring to boil, transfer to oven, cover and cook until meat is very tender, 1 to 1½ hours, stirring occasionally.

Transfer rabbit to serving platter and keep warm. Skim fat from sauce. Bring sauce to boil, then stir in cream, scraping up any browned bits. Boil gently until sauce is reduced to desired consistency (sauce should be smooth). Stir in mustard (do not boil, or mustard will be bitter) and blend well. Season with salt and pepper to taste. Spoon sauce over rabbit. Sprinkle with minced fresh parsley and serve.

Vegetables, Cheese and Pasta

Potato Paprikás Pie

This delightful cold-weather brunch pie can be assembled one day ahead and refrigerated. Let stand at room temperature about 20 minutes to remove chill before baking.

Try to use only imported Hungarian paprika and country bacon; you'll be rewarded with superb dining. Serve with a green salad, a full-bodied red wine and fresh fruit.

6 to 8 servings

Liptauer Pastry (see recipe, page 92)

¾ pound slab or country smoked bacon, chopped
2 medium onions, chopped
2 tablespoons water
2 teaspoons imported sweet Hungarian paprika
1 teaspoon tomato paste
1 teaspoon whole caraway seeds

2½ pounds baking potatoes, peeled, thinly sliced into rounds and parboiled 3 minutes, drained and patted dry
8 ounces cream cheese, crumbled
6 ounces imported Muenster cheese, shredded
2 green onions, minced
Salt and freshly ground pepper

1 egg, beaten (optional)

Generously grease shallow 6-cup baking dish. Roll out ⅔ of pastry on floured surface to thickness of about ⅛ inch. Line dish and chill about 30 minutes.

While pastry is chilling, position rack in lower third of oven and preheat to 400°F. Cook bacon in large skillet over medium heat until crisp. Remove with slotted spoon and drain on paper towels. Pour off all but 2 tablespoons fat. Add onion and cook over high heat 1 to 2 minutes. Reduce heat to low and stir in water, paprika, tomato paste and caraway. Cook, stirring constantly, about 3 minutes. Remove mixture from heat and stir in potatoes, bacon, cheeses, green onion, salt and pepper.

Trim pastry, leaving ½-inch overhang. Spoon in filling, packing tightly. Roll out remaining pastry and cover top of pie. Trim and roll under overhang. Pinch edges together and flute. Brush with beaten egg if desired. Cut several slits to allow steam to escape. Bake 15 minutes. Reduce oven to 350°F and bake until potatoes can be pierced easily with sharp knife inserted through steam slits, 1 to 1¼ hours.

Leek and Cheese Tart

Both leek and sauce can be prepared one day in advance. Assemble tart on serving day.

6 servings

3 cups sliced leeks (white part only), thoroughly rinsed

1 cup milk or double-strength reconstituted nonfat dry milk
½ cup mixture of sliced carrot, celery and onion
1 bay leaf
Pinch of herb or vegetable salt

2 tablespoons vegetable oil (preferably cold-pressed safflower)

1 tablespoon whole wheat pastry flour or unbleached all purpose flour
1½ cups grated Swiss cheese
½ teaspoon dry mustard
2 tablespoons sour cream

1 10-inch baked Cheese Short Pastry shell (see variation in recipe for Basic Short Pastry, page 91)
¼ cup freshly grated Parmesan cheese

Preheat oven to 375°F. Cook leeks in rapidly boiling salted water just until tender, about 2 minutes. Drain well. Pat dry with paper towels and set aside.

Combine milk, carrot mixture, bay leaf and salt in 1-quart saucepan over medium heat and bring to boil. Reduce heat to very low and cook 5 minutes without boiling. Remove from heat.

Combine oil and flour in another medium saucepan and stir over low heat 1 minute. Remove from heat. Strain milk mixture into oil and flour, blending well. Place over medium heat and cook, stirring constantly, until sauce comes to boil. Reduce heat, add ¾ cup Swiss cheese with mustard and stir until cheese is melted. Blend in sour cream.

Spoon about ⅓ of sauce into prepared pastry shell. Sprinkle with leeks and then with remaining Swiss cheese. Cover with remaining sauce. Sprinkle Parmesan over top. Bake until tart is lightly browned, about 10 minutes. Cut into wedges and serve immediately.

Leeks can be cooked 1 day ahead. Bring them to room temperature before assembling tart.

Sauce can be prepared 1 day ahead and stored, covered, in refrigerator. Reheat over low heat before assembling tart.

Spinach Tart with Onion Rings

The filling can be prepared one day ahead, covered and refrigerated.

This spinach tart is based on one of cooking teacher Dione Lucas's most popular creations.

6 servings

Crust
- 2 tablespoons whole wheat breadcrumbs
- 2 tablespoons freshly grated Parmesan cheese
- 1 baked 10-inch Basic Short Pastry shell (see recipe, page 91)

Filling
- 1 pound fresh spinach, thoroughly rinsed
- 5 tablespoons vegetable oil (preferably cold-pressed safflower)
- 1 cup finely chopped yellow onion
- ½ teaspoon finely chopped garlic Herb or vegetable salt
- 3 eggs

- 2 egg yolks
- ½ teaspoon dry mustard Pinch of ground red pepper
- 2¼ cups milk or double-strength reconstituted nonfat dry milk, scalded
- ¼ cup freshly grated Parmesan cheese

Garnish
- 12 to 16 ½-inch-thick onion rings Unbleached all purpose flour or whole wheat pastry flour
- 1 egg, beaten
- ¾ cup (about) whole wheat breadcrumbs Vegetable oil for deep frying (preferably cold-pressed safflower)

For crust: Preheat oven to 350°F. Combine breadcrumbs and cheese and sprinkle over bottom of shell. Set aside.

For filling: Place spinach in bottom of large saucepan and sprinkle with small amount of water. Cover and cook over high heat, turning leaves a few times, until wilted. Transfer to colander and drain well, pressing spinach with back of spoon to remove excess moisture. Chop spinach finely and set aside.

Heat 1 tablespoon oil in medium skillet over low heat. Add onion and garlic and cook 3 minutes, stirring occasionally. Season with salt. Blend in spinach. Remove from heat and set aside.

Combine eggs, egg yolks, mustard and red pepper in medium bowl and whisk until well blended. Add remaining 4 tablespoons oil with milk and mix well. Blend in spinach mixture. Spoon into prepared shell. Sprinkle with 2 tablespoons cheese. Bake until filling is set, about 30 minutes. Remove from oven and sprinkle with remaining cheese. Let cool while preparing garnish.

For garnish: Dust onion rings lightly with flour, shaking off excess. Brush with beaten egg, then coat evenly with crumbs. Pour oil into deep saucepan or deep fryer to depth of 2 to 3 inches and heat to 350°F. Add onion rings in batches and fry until golden brown, about 2 to 3 minutes. Transfer to paper towels using slotted spoon and drain well. Arrange onion rings in overlapping circle around edge of tart. Serve.

Calzoni

Calzoni can be baked ahead and frozen.

Sliced tomatoes dressed with olive oil, lemon juice, minced garlic and chopped fresh basil would be a perfect salad with this Italian turnover. Uncork a robust California Barbera.

Makes 8 calzoni

Dough
- 1 envelope dry yeast
- ¼ cup warm water (105°F to 115°F)
- 4 cups all purpose flour
  Pinch of salt
- 2 tablespoons olive oil
- 1 cup water

Filling
- ½ pound ricotta cheese
- 6 ounces mozzarella cheese, diced

- 1 egg
- ½ cup diced ham
- 1 teaspoon salt
- 1 10-ounce package frozen chopped spinach, cooked, well drained and squeezed dry
- ½ teaspoon dried Italian herbs (basil, oregano and/or rosemary)

For dough: Dissolve yeast in warm water and let stand until foamy, about 10 minutes. Combine flour and salt in large bowl and mix in oil. Add yeast mixture and 1 cup water and stir until dough comes away from bowl *(do not add more water even if dough seems dry).* Turn out onto lightly floured surface and knead until smooth, about 10 minutes, adding flour if necessary. Place in greased bowl, turning to coat entire surface. Cover and let rise until doubled, about 45 minutes.

For filling: Mix all ingredients well.

Punch dough down and divide into 8 equal pieces. Roll each into ball, then flatten and roll each into 6-inch round.

Preheat oven to 450°F. Place ⅛ of filling on half of each circle, leaving border at edges. Fold unfilled half over. Moisten edges with water and pinch to seal. Let rest 10 minutes. Make 2 short slashes in tops, then spray with cold water. Bake until crusts are evenly browned, about 15 to 20 minutes. Serve warm or cold.

Crepes with Sauce Mornay

Crepes can be prepared ahead, cooled, wrapped in plastic and refrigerated for several days, or wrapped in freezer paper or foil and frozen for several weeks. Filled crepes can be refrigerated several days.

Simone Beck inspired this dish.

6 to 8 servings

Crepes (makes 24 6½-inch crepes)
- 1 cup flour
- 2 cups milk, room temperature
- 3 eggs
- 1 egg yolk
- 1 teaspoon salt
- ¼ teaspoon freshly ground pepper
- ⅛ teaspoon freshly grated nutmeg

- 6 tablespoons (¾ stick) butter

Sauce Mornay
- ¼ cup (½ stick) butter

- ¼ cup flour
- 3 cups milk

- 2 egg yolks
- ½ cup whipping cream
- 4 ounces Emmenthaler or Parmesan cheese, finely diced (1 cup)
  Salt, freshly ground pepper and freshly grated nutmeg

For crepes: Place flour in bowl. Add about ⅔ cup of milk a bit at a time, whisking constantly to make smooth paste. Gradually whisk in remaining milk, eggs and egg yolk. Season with salt, pepper and nutmeg. Press through sieve (if there are any lumps) and let stand at room temperature at least 1 hour, or cover and refrigerate overnight.

Melt butter in 6½-inch crepe pan. Let cool slightly, then stir ⅔ of butter into batter, mixing well. Clarify remaining butter and pour into small glass.

Heat pan over medium-high heat. Brush with clarified butter and return to heat until almost smoking. Remove from heat, ladle about 3 tablespoons of batter into one corner of pan, then quickly tilt pan in all directions until bottom is covered with thin layer of batter; pour off any excess.

Return pan to medium-high heat. Loosen edges of crepe using small spatula or knife and cook about 1 minute until bottom of crepe is brown, shaking pan in circle so crepe does not stick. Regulate heat so bottom of crepe develops "craters" and mottled caramel-brown color before it is flipped *(the pan is too hot if batter forms holes as soon as it is poured in; it is too cool if edges of crepe do not color immediately).* Flip or turn crepe over with spatula and cook another minute until second side is brown. Slide out onto plate. Cover with piece of waxed paper. Repeat until all batter is used, brushing pan with additional clarified butter after every 2 or 3 crepes.

For Sauce Mornay: Melt butter in heavy saucepan over low heat. Whisk in flour and let foam 3 minutes without coloring, stirring constantly. Whisk in milk and stir over medium-high heat until sauce comes to boil. Reduce heat and simmer until reduced by ⅓, about 40 minutes, stirring occasionally. Strain.

Mix egg yolks with cream. Slowly whisk in strained sauce. Return to saucepan and bring to boil over medium-high heat, stirring constantly. Remove from heat and stir in all but 3 tablespoons cheese. Add salt, pepper and nutmeg.

To assemble: Preheat oven to 400°F. Butter 9 × 12-inch baking dish. Turn crepes over and spread several tablespoons of sauce on least attractive side of each crepe. Roll up cigar fashion and place seam side down in single layer in baking dish. Pour remaining sauce over top and sprinkle with reserved cheese. Bake until heated through, about 15 minutes. Remove from oven and heat broiler. Run under broiler until cheese is browned, about 1 minute. Let crepes stand for 5 minutes before serving.

Lasagne Verdi e Bianco (Green and White Lasagne)

A hearty dish that can be prepared with or without meat and doubled for a large group. The lasagne can be assembled without the sauce and refrigerated up to three days or frozen up to two months. Pour sauce over top before baking. The sauce can be prepared three days ahead and refrigerated.

10 servings

Herbed Tomato Béchamel Sauce
¼ cup (½ stick) butter
¼ cup all purpose flour
3 tablespoons chopped fresh basil or 1 tablespoon dried, crumbled
¾ teaspoon fresh thyme or ⅛ teaspoon dried, crumbled
Generous pinch of dried oregano
2 cups milk or half and half
1 cup thick tomato puree
3 egg yolks
Salt and freshly ground pepper
Freshly grated nutmeg
1 tablespoon butter, room temperature

Lasagne
¼ cup (½ stick) butter
2 medium onions, finely chopped
3 garlic cloves, minced
½ cup pine nuts or chopped almonds
3 pounds fresh spinach, cooked until wilted, squeezed dry and finely chopped, or 5 10-ounce packages frozen spinach, thawed, squeezed dry and finely chopped

Salt and freshly ground pepper
Freshly grated nutmeg
⅓ cup raisins

1 pound ricotta cheese, drained
½ pound spicy Italian salami, minced (optional)
4 green onions, minced
1 egg yolk
3 tablespoons minced fresh parsley
3 tablespoons fresh basil or 1 tablespoon dried, crumbled
Salt and freshly ground pepper
8 ounces fontinella cheese, shredded
8 ounces Asiago or Parmesan cheese, grated
3 ounces Gruyère or Swiss cheese, shredded

½ to ¾ pound lasagne noodles, cooked al dente, rinsed and drained on paper towels.

For sauce: Melt ¼ cup butter in heavy nonaluminum saucepan over medium-low heat until bubbly. Remove from heat and whisk in flour, basil, thyme and oregano. Cook, stirring constantly, about 3 to 5 minutes (be careful not to let flour brown). Gradually whisk in milk. Increase heat slightly and cook, stirring constantly, until sauce has thickened. Stir in tomato puree. Remove from heat and let cool about 5 minutes. Whisk in egg yolks. Season with salt, pepper and nutmeg to taste. Transfer to storage container. Spread 1 tablespoon butter over sauce to prevent skin from forming. Cover and refrigerate until ready to use.

For lasagne: Melt butter in large nonaluminum skillet over medium heat. Add onion and cook, stirring frequently, until browned and caramelized, about 25 to 30 minutes. Stir in garlic and nuts and cook about 30 seconds. Mix in spinach and cook, stirring frequently, until dry. Remove from heat and season with salt, pepper and nutmeg to taste. Blend in raisins. Set aside and let cool.

Combine ricotta, salami, green onion, egg yolk, parsley, basil and salt and pepper in medium bowl and blend well. Mix fontinella, Asiago and Gruyère cheeses in another medium bowl; reserve 1¼ cups for topping.

Preheat oven to 375°F. Generously butter 9 × 13-inch baking dish or 2 medium baking dishes. Whisk through chilled sauce several times to lighten. Spread thin layer over bottom of prepared dish(es). Cover with layer of pasta. Top with thin layer of spinach. Dot with ricotta mixture and sprinkle with fontinella mixture. Repeat layering, ending with pasta. Pour remaining sauce over lasagne and sprinkle with reserved cheeses. Bake until bubbly and lightly browned, about 45 to 60 minutes. Turn off heat; let lasagne stand in oven 20 minutes before cutting into squares and serving.

For a variation, spread each lasagne noodle with thin layers of spinach and ricotta mixture. Roll each noodle up jelly roll fashion, tucking small stalk of lightly steamed broccoli into each roll. Arrange in bottom of buttered baking dish. Sprinkle with fontinella mixture. Cover and freeze or refrigerate. Pour sauce over pasta rolls just before baking.

5 ❦ Accompaniments

Often it is the little extra touches that make a meal special: the fragrant casserole of vegetables, the piquant condiment or tangy pickle, the homey fruit conserve, the oven-fresh loaf of wholesome bread. And any cook can have such culinary grace notes ready at a moment's notice, since so many accompaniments can be prepared days, weeks or months in advance.

Any vegetable dish that has been cooked until soft—and particularly purees of such familiar root staples as onions, carrots, potatoes and yams—is as good reheated after a day or two of refrigeration as it is freshly cooked. Still other vegetable side dishes gain something from advance preparation: Pickled Herb Carrots (page 71), for example, steep in a mustard marinade, acquiring a tangy savor.

All kinds of condiments, pickles and preserves are by their very nature made-ahead dishes, ready to take down from the cupboard, open and enjoy. They can give spark to virtually every part of a meal. Fresh Basil Pesto (page 75) tossed with pasta, for example, makes a vibrant first course. The Autumn Chutney on page 79, a spicy-sweet blend of mixed fruit, vegetables, jalapeño peppers and brown sugar, makes a perfect relish for a curry or a platter of cold rare roast beef, chicken or ham. Any of the special vinegars on page 76 will lend a marvelous perfume to salads or steamed vegetables. And tangy Lemon Curd (page 82) is superb as a spread for hot biscuits or as a filling for tartlet shells.

Breads and pastries can be handily prepared in stages over a day or so. In fact, bread dough actually develops a finer texture and fuller flavor if one or more of its risings occurs slowly overnight in the refrigerator; and the folds and turns that create the buttery layers of puff pastry (page 91) are facilitated by letting the dough rest and chill for several hours or up to two days. Most breads can also be baked, cooled, wrapped airtight and then frozen for long periods without any sacrifice of quality; defrosted and, if you like, briefly reheated, they will taste as good as if they had come straight from the oven.

 Vegetables

Oregon Baked Lima Beans

Beans can be made up to two days ahead.

12 servings

4 cups dried lima beans

1 pound thickly sliced bacon, diced

5 to 6 tablespoons brown sugar

1 tablespoon dry mustard

1 tablespoon salt

1 teaspoon freshly ground pepper

1 teaspoon ground ginger

1¼ cups boiling water

6 tablespoons molasses

Combine beans with cold water to cover in large saucepan and let soak overnight. Drain well. Cover again with cold water and bring to boil over medium-high heat. Reduce heat and simmer, stirring occasionally, until tender, about 40 to 45 minutes. Drain well.

Preheat oven to 250°F. Transfer beans to 3-quart bean pot or earthenware bowl. Add bacon and stir gently. Combine next 5 ingredients with ¼ cup boiling water and blend well. Stir in molasses. Pour over beans, then add remaining 1 cup boiling water. Cover mixture and bake 3 to 4 hours, adding more hot water if beans seem dry.

Stir through several times. Increase oven temperature to 300°F and bake beans uncovered until tender and brown on top, about 30 to 45 minutes.

White Beans and Tomatoes

A classic complement to lamb or veal, this dish can be prepared up to two days ahead and refrigerated.

4 servings

1 cup dried Great Northern beans

1 medium-size yellow onion, quartered and secured with wooden toothpick

½ carrot, sliced

1 teaspoon finely chopped garlic

1 bay leaf

1 teaspoon sea salt or 2 teaspoons coarse salt

4 tablespoons vegetable oil (preferably cold-pressed safflower)

2 medium-size ripe tomatoes, peeled and sliced
Herb or vegetable salt

2 tablespoons finely chopped fresh basil, thyme or parsley (garnish)

Discard any discolored beans. Rinse remainder under cold running water. Drain well. Transfer to large bowl. Add enough cold water to allow beans to expand at least 2½ times, about 2½ to 3 cups. Let soak at least 8 hours or overnight. (Beans can be quick-soaked. Boil 2 to 3 minutes. Remove from heat, cover and let soak for 1 hour.)

Transfer beans and soaking liquid to heavy large saucepan or Dutch oven. Add onion, carrot, ½ teaspoon garlic, bay leaf and salt and bring to boil over medium-high heat. Reduce heat to low, cover and simmer about 1 hour. Add 2 tablespoons oil, cover and continue cooking until beans are tender, about 30 minutes. Drain and set aside.

Warm remaining oil in heavy large saucepan over low heat. Add remaining garlic and stir 1 minute. Blend in tomatoes. Add salt to taste. Increase heat to medium and cook 5 minutes. Add beans, reduce heat to low and cook 5 minutes. Transfer to serving dish. Sprinkle with basil, thyme or parsley.

Marinated Tomatoes

Tomatoes can be marinated up to three days in advance.

12 servings

1 pint (2 cups) cherry tomatoes
6 tablespoons olive oil
1 tablespoon finely chopped fresh dill or 1½ teaspoons dried dillweed

2 green onions, minced
2 tablespoons minced fresh parsley
Salt and freshly ground pepper

Place tomatoes in lettuce basket or strainer set in deep bowl. Pour boiling water over tomatoes just to cover and let stand 1 minute. Immediately plunge tomatoes into ice water; drain well. Peel off skins and discard. Let tomatoes drain briefly on paper towels. Transfer to serving bowl. Add olive oil, dill, onion, parsley, salt and pepper and toss gently. Cover and refrigerate.

Pickled Herb Carrots

Prepare two to three days before serving.

8 servings

⅔ cup dry white wine
⅔ cup white wine vinegar
½ cup olive oil
1 teaspoon sugar
1 teaspoon salt
5 fresh thyme sprigs, minced, or ½ teaspoon dried, crumbled
3 fresh parsley sprigs, minced

1 garlic clove, minced
1 bay leaf
⅛ teaspoon ground red pepper
⅔ cup water
1 pound tender young carrots, cut into ¼-inch julienne
1½ tablespoons Dijon mustard

Combine wine, vinegar, oil, sugar, salt, thyme, parsley, garlic, bay leaf and pepper in large skillet. Stir in ⅔ cup water. Place over medium-high heat and bring to boil. Add carrots and continue boiling until carrots are just crisp-tender, 20 to 25 minutes. Stir in mustard, blending thoroughly. Cover and set aside. Let marinate in cool place 2 to 3 days. Serve hot or cold.

Estouffade of Carrots and Onions

Estouffade can be prepared up to three days in advance and reheated.

4 to 5 servings

12 small white onions (preferably boiling onions), unpeeled

1 cup diced meaty salt pork

2 tablespoons (¼ stick) butter

1½ teaspoons sugar
4 to 6 small carrots, cut into ¾-inch cubes

Pinch of thyme
Salt and freshly ground pepper
½ to ¾ cup brown stock or beef bouillon
1 bay leaf

Minced parsley (garnish)

Drop onions into rapidly boiling salted water and cook 5 minutes. Drain well. When cool enough to handle, peel and set aside.

Drop salt pork into rapidly boiling water and blanch 3 minutes. Drain in colander and dry well on paper towels.

Melt butter in medium saucepan over medium heat. Add salt pork and sauté until almost crisp. Remove with slotted spoon and set aside.

Add onions to saucepan and sauté 3 minutes, tossing them in the fat until lightly browned (*the onions will not brown evenly*). Sprinkle with half the sugar, cover partially and continue cooking over medium-low heat, shaking constantly until onions are lightly caramelized. Add carrot, salt pork, thyme, salt and pepper. Mix in stock and remaining sugar. Bury bay leaf in mixture. Cover and simmer 20 minutes, or until vegetables are tender.

Remove lid, increase heat and continue cooking, shaking pan to prevent sticking, until all stock has evaporated. Taste and correct seasoning. Discard bay leaf. Transfer to bowl, sprinkle with minced parsley and serve immediately.

For a variation, 6 to 8 cubed mushrooms sautéed separately in 2 tablespoons butter may be added just before serving.

Pommes Dauphine

Potato mixture can be prepared and refrigerated one day before deep frying. Pommes can be cooked 45 minutes before serving.

8 servings

½ cup (1 stick) plus 1 tablespoon unsalted butter
1 cup cold water
2 teaspoons salt
1 cup all purpose flour
4 eggs

Freshly grated nutmeg
2 large potatoes (about), cooked and mashed

Oil for deep frying

Combine butter, water and salt in large saucepan. Place over low heat and stir until butter is melted. Remove from heat and stir in flour. Return to heat and stir constantly to let mixture dry, about 20 seconds. Add eggs 2 at a time and beat on high speed of electric mixer. Season with nutmeg to taste. Measure 2½ cups potatoes and add to mixture, beating well. *(Can be prepared 1 day ahead to this point and refrigerated.)*

Add oil to depth of 3 inches in deep fryer or pot and heat to 375°F. Add potato mixture by small rounded tablespoons and fry until golden brown. Remove with slotted spoon and drain on paper towels. Keep warm on paper-towel-lined platter (do not let sides touch) until ready to serve.

Potato and Carrot Puree au Gratin

This vegetable dish can be prepared one day ahead and refrigerated. Bring to room temperature and reheat.

4 servings

4 medium potatoes (about 1½ pounds total), scrubbed and quartered
4 large carrots (about 1 pound), peeled and cut into large pieces
1 egg
6 tablespoons freshly grated Parmesan cheese

2 tablespoons (¼ stick) unsalted butter
2 tablespoons sour cream
½ teaspoon dry mustard
Ground red pepper
Herb or vegetable salt (optional)

Butter 9-inch pie plate or 1½-quart baking dish. Steam or boil potatoes and carrots until tender, about 18 to 20 minutes. Remove potato skins and discard. Press potatoes and carrots through sieve or mash with potato masher. Transfer to large bowl of electric mixer. Add egg, 3 tablespoons Parmesan, 1 tablespoon butter, sour cream, mustard, ground red pepper and herb salt to taste. Mix well.

Preheat broiler. Transfer mixture to prepared baking dish. Sprinkle remaining Parmesan over and dot with remaining 1 tablespoon butter. Broil until top is brown. Serve immediately.

Casserole of Potatoes and Tomatoes

Casserole can be assembled ahead of time and refrigerated. Bake just before serving.

4 to 6 servings

4 large baking potatoes (about ½ pound each), scrubbed and quartered
1 egg
2 tablespoons light vegetable oil (preferably cold-pressed safflower)
  Ground red pepper
  Herb or vegetable salt (optional)

2 tablespoons olive oil (preferably cold-pressed)
½ teaspoon finely chopped garlic

3 large ripe tomatoes, peeled and thickly sliced
  Freshly ground white pepper
½ to 1 teaspoon dried basil, crumbled

5 tablespoons freshly grated Parmesan cheese
2 tablespoons dry whole wheat breadcrumbs

Steam or boil potatoes until tender, about 18 to 20 minutes. Remove potato skins and discard. Transfer potatoes to large bowl of electric mixer and beat until smooth. Add egg, 1 tablespoon vegetable oil and ground red pepper to taste. Mix well. Season with herb salt to taste. Set aside.

Combine olive oil and garlic in large skillet. Cook over low heat, stirring constantly, 1 minute. Add sliced tomato. Increase heat to medium and cook until tomatoes have rendered juices, 3 to 4 minutes. Remove tomato from pan and set aside. Increase heat to high and boil juices until thickened and reduced, about 2 to 3 minutes. Season sauce with herb salt and white pepper to taste. Stir in basil.

Preheat oven to 350°F. Oil 1½-quart ovenproof glass baking dish. Spread half of potato puree in bottom of prepared dish. Add tomato slices and top with sauce. Sprinkle 1 tablespoon Parmesan over sauce. Top with remaining potato puree. Sprinkle with breadcrumbs and remaining Parmesan. Drizzle remaining oil over cheese. *(Casserole can be prepared ahead to this point and refrigerated. Bring to room temperature before baking.)* Bake 45 minutes.

Sweet Potatoes Duchesse

Sweet potatoes can be prepared in advance and refrigerated. Brown lightly before serving.

2 servings

2 small to medium sweet potatoes, peeled and quartered
2 tablespoons (¼ stick) butter, room temperature

1 egg yolk
⅛ teaspoon mace
⅛ teaspoon freshly grated nutmeg
  Salt

Boil sweet potatoes in salted water until tender. Drain, return to pan and shake over high heat for a few seconds to evaporate any remaining moisture. Transfer to bowl and mash. Using electric mixer, beat in butter until smooth. With mixer running, add yolk and spices and whip at high speed until fluffy. Add salt to taste.

Using pastry bag fitted with open star tube, pipe potato mixture around edge of ovenproof platter. Set aside to cool. Cover loosely and refrigerate.

About 30 minutes before serving, remove platter from refrigerator and bring mixture to room temperature. Preheat broiler. Five minutes before serving, run platter under broiler until peaks and ridges of mixture are lightly browned, watching carefully.

Dried Legume Puree

Puree can be prepared ahead and frozen in air-tight container.

Any dried legume makes an excellent puree. Use this recipe as a guide.

Makes 2 to 2½ cups

1 cup dried legumes (dried beans, peas or lentils)

1 medium-size yellow onion, quartered and secured with wooden pick

½ carrot, sliced

½ teaspoon chopped fresh garlic

1 bay leaf

1 teaspoon sea salt or 2 teaspoons coarse salt

4 tablespoons vegetable oil

1 tablespoon all purpose flour (optional)

3 tablespoons sour cream or plain yogurt

Herb or vegetable salt

Discard any discolored legumes. Rinse remainder under cold running water. Drain well. Transfer to large bowl. Add enough cold water to allow legumes to expand at least 2½ times, about 2½ to 3 cups. Let soak at least 8 hours or overnight. (Legumes can be quick-soaked. Boil 2 to 3 minutes. Remove from heat, cover and let soak 1 hour.)

Drain legumes well, reserving soaking liquid. Transfer legumes to heavy large saucepan. Add liquid to cover (and additional water if necessary). Add onion, carrot, garlic, bay leaf and sea salt and bring to boil over medium-high heat. Reduce heat to low, cover tightly and simmer about 1 hour. Add 2 tablespoons oil, cover and cook until legumes are tender, about 30 minutes.

Drain legumes well. Discard onion, carrot and bay leaf. Puree legumes with a little cooking liquid in processor or blender. Warm remaining oil in heavy large saucepan over low heat. Stir in flour if thicker puree is desired. Add legume puree and sour cream or yogurt and blend well. Add herb salt to taste. Stir until heated through, 10 minutes.

Rice and Rye Pilaf

The rye or whole wheat berries can be cooked up to two days in advance. Prepare pilaf before serving.

25 servings

1 cup rye or whole wheat berries

¾ cup (1½ sticks) butter

1 large onion, chopped

4 cups long-grain converted rice

6 cups chicken broth (preferably homemade)

1 teaspoon salt

Bring 1 cup water to simmer in medium saucepan over low heat. Add rye or whole wheat berries, cover and cook until all water is absorbed, about 45 minutes. Set aside. *(Can be prepared ahead and refrigerated.)*

One hour before serving, melt butter in large skillet over medium-high heat. Add onion and sauté until transparent. Mix in rice, stirring until sizzling. Add broth, cooked rye and salt and bring to boil. Reduce heat, cover and simmer 20 minutes. Remove from heat, transfer to chafing dish or top of double boiler and keep warm until ready to serve.

Condiments, Pickles and Preserves

Fresh Basil Pesto

Pesto will keep up to 3 months in the refrigerator, indefinitely in the freezer.

Make large quantities while fresh basil leaves are at their prime.

Makes 1⅔ cups

2 cups packed fresh basil leaves
2 large garlic cloves
½ cup pine nuts
¾ cup freshly grated Parmesan or Romano cheese
⅔ cup olive oil

With mortar and pestle: Mince basil leaves finely. Transfer to mortar and crush to fine paste. Add garlic and work into paste. Gradually add pine nuts and crush until smooth. Blend in cheese. Add olive oil to mixture in slow steady stream, stirring constantly.

With processor: Combine basil and garlic in work bowl and blend to fine paste, scraping down sides of bowl as necessary. Add pine nuts and cheese and process until smooth. With machine running, pour olive oil through feed tube in slow steady stream and mix until smooth and creamy; if pesto is too thick, gradually pour up to ¼ cup warm water through feed tube with machine running.

Transfer pesto to jar. Cover surface of pesto with film of olive oil about ⅛ inch thick. Seal jar with tight-fitting lid. Refrigerate or freeze. Stir oil into pesto before using.

Hot Pepper Sauce

This rich, assertive sauce can be prepared up to one week ahead, covered tightly and refrigerated. It goes well with fried won ton or other dumplings with robust character.

Makes about ⅓ cup

1 teaspoon minced fresh ginger
1 teaspoon minced fresh garlic
1 tablespoon hoisin sauce
1 tablespoon dark soy sauce
1½ teaspoons hot brown bean sauce (also known as hot bean sauce)
1½ teaspoons water
¾ teaspoon brown bean sauce (also known as ground bean sauce)
½ teaspoon sugar
1½ tablespoons corn oil
2 tablespoons dried chili peppers, soaked in water, drained and chopped
1½ teaspoons distilled white vinegar
¼ teaspoon sesame oil

Mix ginger and garlic in small bowl. Combine hoisin, soy sauce, hot bean sauce, water, brown bean sauce and sugar in another bowl and mix well.

Heat oil in wok. Add ginger and garlic and stir-fry 10 seconds. Add chili peppers and stir-fry 10 seconds. Blend in hoisin mixture and stir-fry 10 seconds. Add vinegar and stir-fry 5 seconds. Mix in sesame oil. Remove from heat. Cool.

Spiced Oil

Prepare at least ten days ahead; store in cool, dark area. Use in dressings, marinades or for basting.

Makes 1 quart

12 whole coriander seeds, crushed
6 whole allspice berries
5 or 6 whole cloves
3 garlic cloves, split
2 whole cinnamon sticks
1 or 2 small hot chilies
1 ¼-inch-thick slice fresh ginger
Peanut or vegetable oil

Place spices and seasoning in 1-quart glass bottle. Add oil almost to fill. Cap.

Special Herbed Olive Oil

Store in cool, dark area for ten days before using. Use in vinaigrettes, for basting and in marinades.

Makes 1 quart

6 fresh rosemary branches
6 whole black peppercorns
3 garlic cloves, split
3 bay leaves

2 fresh thyme branches
2 long sprigs fresh oregano
Olive oil

Place herbs and seasoning in 1-quart glass bottle. Add olive oil almost to fill. Cap.

Lemon-Garlic-Mint Vinegar

Prepare vinegar about ten days ahead. Use in marinades for fish or poultry.

Makes 1 quart

4 long, leafy fresh mint sprigs
3 large garlic cloves, split
1 ¼-inch-wide spiral of lemon peel

1 quart red or white wine vinegar, room temperature

Place mint, garlic and lemon peel in a tall 1-quart glass bottle. Pour vinegar over almost to fill. Cap and seal.

Fresh Fruit Vinegar

This fragrant vinegar can be stored in refrigerator for up to three months. Use in fruit salads, over steamed greens, as a dressing for cabbage, or for basting.

Makes about 2½ quarts

6 cups fresh strawberries, raspberries or peaches
1 quart white wine vinegar

4 cups sugar

Place fruit in 3-quart glass bowl and crush with potato masher. Add vinegar, cover tightly and let stand in cool area for at least 24 hours.

Pour through strainer into large nonaluminum pot, pressing to extract as much fruit pulp and juice as possible (you should get 6 cups). Add sugar. Stirring constantly, bring to a boil. Reduce heat and simmer, stirring, exactly 5 minutes. Let cool. Pour into glass containers and cap tightly.

Spiced Vinegar

Store in cool, dry area for up to 4 months before using. Use in pickles and marinades.

Makes 1 quart

12 whole coriander seeds
6 whole cloves
6 whole allspice berries
1 large or 2 small whole cinnamon sticks

1 dried chili, split (discard seeds, if desired)
1 ¼-inch-thick slice fresh ginger
1 quart red wine vinegar or cider vinegar, warmed

Place spices and seasoning in 1-quart glass bottle. Pour vinegar over almost to fill. Cap and seal.

Tarragon or Dill Vinegar

Allow to infuse two weeks before using.

Makes 1 quart

1 cup (about) long sprigs of fresh tarragon or dill

1 quart white wine vinegar, room temperature

Place herbs in tall 1-quart glass bottle. Pour vinegar over almost to fill. Cap bottle and seal.

🍎 Herb-Flavored Vinegar Tips

Vinegar has a special ability to draw out the fragrant goodness from fresh herbs and suspend them in sweetly aromatic infusions. Add a branch of any fresh herb—or a mixture of several—to good quality wine vinegar and let it mellow. The resulting tarragon, basil or mixed bouquet vinegar can be used in marinades for meat, to dress salads and to flavor cooked vegetables.

- Herb-flavored vinegars should infuse in a sunny spot but never in direct sunlight.
- After infusion, store flavored vinegars in a cool, dark place. They will keep for up to six months.
- Heat vinegar to a simmer before pouring over dry herbs; do not boil.
- Bottles may be purchased from specialty shops, or you can save wine bottles and fill them with flavored oils and vinegars. White or rosé bottles are best because they are usually clear. Wash and dry well before reusing.
- To cap, use bottles with clamp-type porcelain tops. New corks, plastic push-in corks and screw-on caps work well.
- For an especially impressive gift, seal tops with wax by this simple method. Melt brightly colored sealing wax or candle wax in a small frozen juice can set into a pan of hot water. Run a length of ribbon up the side of the bottle and over the top. Turn bottle upside down and lower into hot wax about two to three inches deep. Let wax harden. To break the seal, pull up on ribbon.

Pickled Mustard Greens (Suen Gai Choy)

This delicacy can be kept for several months in the refrigerator.

Makes two 1-quart jars

3 cups water
1 cup sugar
⅔ cup cider vinegar
4 teaspoons salt

4 pounds mustard greens (about)
4 slices fresh ginger (about the size of a quarter)

Combine first 4 ingredients in medium saucepan and bring to boil over high heat. Reduce heat and simmer several minutes, stirring once or twice, until sugar and salt are dissolved. Set aside to cool.

Break side branches from center stalk of greens; discard leaves. Rinse branches and cut into 1- to 1½-inch chunks. Blanch in boiling water 1 minute. Rinse under cold water, drain well and let cool.

Divide greens evenly between 2 1-quart glass jars and place 2 slices fresh ginger in each. Fill jars with cooled vinegar mixture. Cover and refrigerate 1 week before using. Serve as a side dish or as hors d'oeuvres.

Broccoli or celery cabbage (available at oriental supermarkets) can be substituted for mustard greens.

Toorshi (Pickled Vegetables)

Toorshi should be prepared at least one to two weeks ahead. It will keep indefinitely if well sealed and stored in cool, dark place.

Makes 4 quarts

2 quarts water
1 quart white vinegar
⅓ cup coarse salt

12 celery stalks, peeled and sliced into thin sticks about 3 inches long
6 carrots, peeled and sliced into thin sticks about 3 inches long

1 pound cauliflower, separated into florets
1 medium head cabbage, cut into small wedges (about 2 inches)
12 to 16 garlic cloves, peeled

Sterilize 4 1-quart jars. Combine water, vinegar and salt in large saucepan and bring to full boil; keep hot.

Divide vegetables and garlic among jars. Add boiling brine, filling to within ½ inch of top. Seal and store for at least 1 to 2 weeks before serving.

Vegetables also can be layered in a crock. Weight with plate to keep vegetables submerged in brine and store in refrigerator.

Vinegared Fruits

Fruits must be prepared ahead and allowed to stand two to three days.

Serve with pot roast, pork or game.

Makes about 3 pints

2 cups sugar
1 cup water
½ cup Spiced Vinegar (see recipe, page 76)
3 ¼-inch-thick slices fresh ginger

1 to 2 cinnamon sticks, broken into pieces
2 pounds (about) Italian plums
1 pound pitted bing cherries, preferably fresh

Sterilize widemouthed pint jars. Remove from heat and keep warm.

Combine sugar, water, vinegar and ginger in large saucepan over medium-high heat. Add cinnamon sticks to taste and bring to boil. Cook until consistency of medium-heavy syrup, about 8 to 10 minutes. Add whole fruits and cook just until skins begin to split.

Ladle fruits into jars. Add syrup, filling to rim. Divide cinnamon sticks among jars. Seal. Let stand in cool, dark area 2 to 3 days before serving.

Ginger Pear Pickles

These pickles can be prepared ahead and refrigerated up to three weeks.

12 servings

15 medium pears, peeled, cored, seeded and quartered
4 cups (1 quart) water
2 tablespoons white vinegar

5 cups sugar
3 cups white vinegar
1 cup water

1 cup apple juice
1 cup thinly sliced, peeled fresh ginger (reserve peel)
6 cinnamon sticks
¼ cup whole cloves
2 limes, thinly sliced

Combine pears, water and 2 tablespoons vinegar in large bowl and let stand for 10 minutes.

Combine sugar, 3 cups vinegar, water, apple juice and ginger in large saucepan and bring to boil over high heat. Tie ginger peel, cinnamon sticks, cloves and lime in cheesecloth and add to saucepan. Cover and boil 8 to 10 minutes. Drain pears well. Add to sugar mixture and continue boiling until pears are translucent, about 10 minutes. Transfer pears and syrup to large bowl. Let cool slightly, then cover and refrigerate until well chilled. Remove pears from syrup using slotted spoon and arrange in serving bowl. Remove spices from syrup (add to pears if desired). Pour syrup over pears.

Cranberry Apple Relish

An old family recipe, this relish keeps indefinitely in refrigerator.

Makes about 9 cups

2 pounds (8 cups) whole cranberries, preferably fresh, coarsely chopped
4 cups peeled, quartered and cored medium apples, coarsely chopped
3½ cups sugar

2 cups orange marmalade
2 cups coarsely chopped walnuts, toasted
⅓ cup fresh lemon juice
Orange baskets (optional)

Combine all ingredients in large mixing bowl. Cover and refrigerate until ready to use. Serve in hollowed-out orange halves, if desired.

Green Tomato Chutney

Prepare in advance and store in cool, dark place.

Makes about 1½ quarts

4 pounds (about) green tomatoes, cut into ½-inch cubes (12 cups chopped)
1 pound brown sugar
1 pint (2 cups) vinegar (cider, white wine or spiced)
1 tablespoon salt

1 medium to large onion, chopped
1 tablespoon curry powder
2 heaping teaspoons allspice
2 heaping teaspoons mustard seed
1 heaping teaspoon ground ginger
1 teaspoon cracked black pepper
½ teaspoon chili powder (optional)

Prepare jars. Combine tomatoes, sugar and vinegar in Dutch oven or other large kettle. Cook over low heat, stirring frequently until sugar is dissolved. Add remaining ingredients and blend well. Increase heat and simmer until thick, about 1½ to 2 hours, stirring frequently and watching carefully to prevent burning. Ladle into hot sterilized jars to within ½ inch of top and seal. Process 5 minutes in boiling water bath. Remove from water and let cool. Test for seal.

Autumn Chutney

Chutney can be made ahead and stored in cool, dark place.

Makes about 11 half-pint jars

3 medium limes, quartered
4 jalapeño peppers
3 pounds firm ripe tomatoes, chopped
3 pounds brown sugar
2 pounds apples, peeled, cored and chopped
2 pounds pears, peeled, cored and chopped
2 medium peaches, halved, pitted and chopped

1 red bell pepper, seeded and chopped
½ pound dark raisins
½ pound golden raisins
1½ pints (3 cups) vinegar
1 tablespoon salt
2 teaspoons mustard seed
2 teaspoons garam masala or curry powder
1 teaspoon turmeric

Prepare jars. Finely chop limes with peppers in processor or blender. Transfer to Dutch oven or other large kettle. Add remaining ingredients and blend. Bring to boil over medium heat, stirring frequently. Reduce heat and simmer until dark and thick, about 2 hours, stirring often and watching carefully to prevent mixture from burning. Ladle into hot sterilized jars to within ½ inch of top and seal. Process 5 minutes in boiling water bath. Remove from water and let stand until cooled. Test for seal.

Plum-Onion Conserve

Conserve can be refrigerated up to four days and frozen up to four months.

Serve on chunks of snappy cheddar cheese for a tangy appetizer or halve fresh plums and fill with conserve as an attractive relish with cold meats.

Makes about 2 cups

3 tablespoons vegetable oil
1 tablespoon butter
4 large onions, thinly sliced
1 teaspoon sugar
¼ teaspoon salt

1 pound underripe purple plums, unpeeled, pitted and chopped
2 tablespoons (about) sugar
1 tablespoon Spanish Sherry wine vinegar

Combine oil, butter and onion in heavy large saucepan. Cover and cook over low heat 1 hour. Stir in 1 teaspoon sugar with salt. Cover and cook another hour, stirring to prevent sticking.

Add plums, sugar and vinegar to onion and cook uncovered over low heat until thick, about 40 minutes. Let cool and refrigerate. Serve conserve chilled or at room temperature.

For variation, mix Plum-Onion Conserve and 1½ pounds grated sharp cheddar cheese in processor until well blended. Shape into cylinder and serve with sesame crackers.

Lime Marmalade

Can be stored in cool, dark place.

The simmered fruit should be boiled with sugar just to the setting point. If it is cooked too long, the result will be a thick syrup with hard chunks of peel.

Makes about 4 half-pint jars

1¼ pounds limes (about 9 limes)
3½ cups water

4½ cups sugar

Chill a small plate. Prepare jars. Wash limes. Carefully remove peel and cut into very fine shreds. Remove pith and membrane and place in washed cheesecloth or muslin. Thinly slice limes and remove pits *(you need 2 cups sliced fruit)*; add pits to cheesecloth and tie securely. Combine lime, peel, cheesecloth bag and water in heavy large saucepan and bring to boil. Reduce heat and simmer 1½ hours.

Remove bag, squeezing liquid into pan before discarding. Add sugar, stirring until dissolved. Increase heat and bring to hard boil. Let boil until setting point is reached, about 15 minutes. Remove from heat. Spoon small amount onto chilled plate and refrigerate. If it stiffens after 1 minute, it is done; if not, return to boil briefly and test again. Pour into hot sterilized jars to within ¼ inch of top and seal. Process 5 minutes in boiling water bath. Remove from water and let stand undisturbed until cooled. Test for seal.

Mushroom Marmalade Sauce with Fresh Ginger
(Sauce de Marmelade aux Champignons et au Gingembre)

Can be refrigerated up to several weeks. Serve with meats and poultry.

Makes 5 cups

2 pounds firm white mushrooms, thinly sliced
1 tablespoon salt

2 tablespoons (¼ stick) unsalted butter

1 tablespoon fresh lemon juice
4½ cups sugar
2 teaspoons minced fresh ginger
6 ounces liquid fruit pectin
½ teaspoon vanilla

Combine mushrooms and salt in plastic bag and shake gently to distribute salt. Refrigerate 12 hours or overnight, shaking bag occasionally.

Place mushrooms in strainer set over a bowl and press gently to extract at least 1½ cups of mushroom liquid. Pour liquid into heavy 2-quart saucepan and simmer over medium-high heat until reduced to 2 tablespoons.

Meanwhile, melt butter with lemon juice in large skillet over medium-high heat. Add drained mushroom slices and cook *without browning* until all moisture appears to be cooked away, about 8 minutes (stir gently with wooden spoon to avoid damaging slices). Add with sugar and ginger to reduced liquid. Cook over medium-high heat, lifting ingredients with wooden spoon until sugar begins to melt and mixture becomes liquid. Bring to full rolling boil over high heat for 1 minute, stirring occasionally. Remove from heat and immediately stir in pectin and vanilla. Ladle gently into sterilized jars, leaving ⅛ inch at top. Wipe top and threads of jars with damp cloth. Seal with lids following manufacturer's directions.

Blackberry Jam

Can be stored in cool, dark place.

Makes about 5 half-pint jars

4 cups blackberries
4 cups sugar

2 ounces blackberry liqueur or brandy

Combine all ingredients in large deep saucepan. Bring to full rolling boil over medium-high heat, stirring constantly, and cook until very thick, about 20 to 30 minutes. Ladle into sterilized jars and seal with paraffin or canning lids.

Dried Apricot Jam

Can be stored in cool, dark place.

Makes about 8 half-pint jars

1½ pounds dried apricots, quartered
2 quarts water

4 pounds sugar

2 ounces blanched, halved almonds
Juice of 1 large lemon

Rinse apricots. Combine with water in medium bowl. Cover and let stand at room temperature for 48 hours.

Prepare jars. Turn undrained apricots into Dutch oven or other large kettle and bring slowly to boil. Add sugar and stir until dissolved. Let boil until apricots are plump and mixture is thick, about 40 minutes to 1 hour, adding nuts and lemon juice during last 10 minutes of cooking time. Pour jam into hot sterilized jars to within ¼ inch of top and seal. Process 5 minutes in boiling water bath. Remove from water and let stand undisturbed until cooled. Test for seal.

Pomegranate Jelly

Can be stored in cool, dark place.

Makes about 4 one-pint jars

15 to 18 very ripe large pomegranates

7½ cups sugar
6 ounces Certo liquid fruit pectin

Seed pomegranates, making sure no yellow membrane remains. Put seeds through food mill to extract juice (there should be about 5 cups). Cover and refrigerate juice overnight.

Carefully pour juice into large deep saucepan *(pulp will have settled overnight to bottom of container and should be discarded)*. Add sugar and bring to full rolling boil, stirring frequently. Add pectin and continue boiling 1 minute longer, stirring constantly. Remove from heat and skim off foam. Pour into sterilized jars and seal with lids.

Jalapeño Jelly

Can be stored in cool, dark place. For a snappy appetizer, try this on top of crackers spread with cream cheese.

Makes about 6 to 7 half-pint jars

3 medium green peppers, seeded and coarsely chopped
2 2-inch jalapeño peppers, seeded and coarsely chopped

1½ cups distilled white vinegar
6½ cups sugar
1 teaspoon cayenne pepper
6 ounces Certo liquid fruit pectin

Combine peppers in food processor or blender and puree. Add 1 cup vinegar and blend thoroughly. Transfer to large deep saucepan and add remaining vinegar, sugar and cayenne, blending well. Bring to full rolling boil, stirring frequently. Stir in pectin and continue boiling 1 minute longer, stirring constantly. Remove from heat and skim off foam. Pour into sterilized jars and seal.

Lemon Curd

Can be stored up to two months. Spread on English muffins, or use as a cake or pie filling.

Makes about 4 half-pint jars

½ cup (1 stick) butter
1½ cups sugar
1¼ cups strained fresh lemon juice

4 eggs
2 tablespoons grated lemon zest

Melt butter in top of double boiler over simmering water. Add remaining ingredients and blend well. Continue cooking, stirring frequently, until thick and smooth, about 25 to 30 minutes. Ladle into sterilized jars and seal with lids.

Honey Apricot Spread

Spread can be refrigerated two to three weeks.

Makes about 2 cups

2¼ cups dried apricots
1¼ cups honey
1 teaspoon finely chopped lemon peel

1 teaspoon finely chopped orange peel
½ cup chopped fresh pineapple

Cook apricots in enough boiling water to cover for 5 minutes. Drain and let cool slightly. With machine running on medium speed, add apricots to blender a few at a time, mixing well. Add honey in slow steady stream (increasing speed if necessary), blending until mixture is thick and creamy (small pieces of apricot should remain). Transfer to small bowl. Stir in chopped peel. Refrigerate at least 24 hours. Blend in pineapple. Cover and refrigerate until ready to serve.

Breads and Pastries

Classic French Bread

For the best French bread, allow the dough to mature slowly. After baking, the bread can be refrigerated up to two days.

Makes 2 loaves

2½ cups cool water (about 50°F)
2½ cups unbleached all purpose flour (10 ounces)
2½ teaspoons dry yeast

3 to 3½ cups unbleached all purpose flour (12 to 14 ounces)

2½ teaspoons salt

Cornmeal

Combine water, 2½ cups flour and yeast in processor and mix 30 seconds (or beat by hand 2 minutes). Transfer to large bowl. Cover with plastic wrap and let stand at room temperature for about 4 to 5 hours.

Lightly grease large bowl. Add 3 cups flour and salt to yeast mixture, blending well. Stir in enough additional flour to make soft, slightly sticky dough. Knead until dough is very elastic, adding more flour as necessary, about 15 minutes. Transfer to prepared bowl, turning to coat entire surface. Cover with plastic wrap and let rise until 2½ times original bulk, about 3 to 4 hours. Press down on dough using palm of hand. *(Dough can be prepared ahead to this point, covered and refrigerated overnight. Adjust time for second rising for chilled dough.)*

Cover dough and let rise again until 2½ times original bulk, 2½ to 3 hours.

Generously sprinkle flat baking sheet or peel with cornmeal. Press dough down using palms of hands. Turn out onto lightly floured surface. Divide dough in half. Pat each into oval. Fold each in half lengthwise, pressing edges together. Flatten slightly and fold lengthwise again. Arrange seam side down on work surface. Using sides of hands, stretch, smooth and shape dough into taut cylinder. Starting at center of each cylinder, gently stretch until each loaf is about 13 inches long. Arrange loaves on prepared baking sheet, spacing about 6 inches apart. Sprinkle lightly with flour. Cover loaves with towel and let rise at room temperature until more than doubled in volume, approximately 2 to 3 hours.

Arrange quarry tiles on center rack of oven and preheat to 450°F. Place broiler pan on lowest rack. Pour 1 cup water into broiler pan. Generously sprinkle tiles with cornmeal. Cut 4 horizontal slits in top of each loaf using razor or very sharp knife. Slide loaves from baking sheet onto hot tiles. Bake 15 minutes. Remove broiler pan from oven. Continue baking loaves until bottoms sound hollow when tapped, about 20 minutes. Cool on rack at least 1 hour before slicing.

Loaves can be wrapped tightly and refrigerated 1 to 2 days. Reheat briefly in 400°F oven before serving.

Hard Rolls

Hard Rolls can be pre-pared ahead and frozen.

Makes 6 rolls

6 tablespoons warm water (105°F to 115°F)
1 envelope dry yeast
1 teaspoon sugar
3½ to 4 cups flour (use mixture of half gluten flour and half unbleached all purpose flour)

1¼ cups warm water (105°F to 115°F)
1½ teaspoons salt

1 egg beaten with 1 teaspoon water

Generously grease large mixing bowl and baking sheet. Set aside. Combine 6 tablespoons warm water with yeast and sugar in another large bowl and stir until yeast is dissolved. Let stand until foamy and proofed, about 10 minutes. Add flours to yeast mixture alternately with remaining warm water, stirring until well blended. Mix in salt.

Turn dough out onto floured surface and knead until dough is smooth and elastic, about 10 to 12 minutes (or mix with dough hook of electric mixer 6 minutes). Form into ball. Transfer to greased bowl, turning to coat entire surface. Cover lightly and let stand in warm draft-free area (85°F) until doubled in volume, about 1½ to 2 hours.

Punch dough down. Cover and let stand in warm draft-free area 15 minutes. Transfer dough to floured surface. Cut into six 5-ounce pieces (use scale to make sure pieces are of equal weight). Roll into balls. Cover and let stand in warm draft-free area until doubled, 45 minutes to 1 hour (tops will get crusty and dry).

Flatten each ball and fold in half, crusty side in. Roll in palms of hands to form "petit pain," about 5½ × 1½ inches, tapering ends. Arrange rolls seam side down on prepared baking sheet, spacing 2 inches apart. Cover and let stand in warm draft-free area until doubled, about 1 hour.

Preheat oven to 425°F. Position one rack in center of oven and one in lower third. Place large shallow pan of water on lower rack. Make slash ½ inch deep and 4 inches long down center of each roll. Brush gently with egg. Set baking sheet on center oven rack and bake, spraying rolls frequently with water to form crisp crust, about 20 minutes. Transfer to rack to cool.

Benne Biscuits

Biscuits can be made up to one month ahead.

Makes about 35 dozen tiny biscuits

¾ cup benne seed (unhulled sesame seed)*

Dough for 9-inch pie crust
5 ounces extra sharp cheddar cheese, grated

½ teaspoon freshly ground red pepper
1 to 2 teaspoons ice water (optional)

Salt

Preheat oven to 350°F. Arrange seed in shallow layer in large pan. Roast 30 minutes, stirring every 10 minutes. Taste seed; if not toasted, continue roasting, testing every 5 minutes (not more than 15 minutes). Do not overtoast or seed will be bitter. Retain oven temperature at 350°F.

Combine dough, cheese and ground red pepper in large bowl and blend well. Stir in benne seed. If dough is too dry to incorporate seed, add 1 to 2 teaspoons ice water and mix well.

Divide dough in half. Turn half out onto lightly floured surface or pastry cloth and pat gently to flatten slightly. Lightly flour top of dough. Roll out to thickness of ⅛ inch. Using sharp knife or fluted pastry wheel, cut dough into ⅝-inch squares. Transfer squares to ungreased baking sheet. Bake just until lightly browned, about 4 minutes. Cool 5 minutes. Repeat with remaining dough. Sprinkle biscuits with salt before serving. *(Can be prepared up to 1 month ahead. Store in container with tight-fitting lid in cool, dark place. Reheat for several minutes in 350°F oven.)*

*Unhulled sesame seed is available at natural foods stores. Do not substitute white sesame seed, which becomes oily when heated and will not toast properly.

Whole Wheat Quick Bread

This quick bread can be made in advance and frozen. Serve with Honey Apricot Spread (see recipe, page 82) and a jasmine tea.

Makes 1 9 × 5-inch loaf

2 cups whole wheat flour
¼ cup soy flour, sifted
¼ cup bran flakes
¼ cup cracked wheat cereal or wheat germ
¼ cup nonfat dry milk
1 teaspoon baking soda
1 teaspoon baking powder (without aluminum salts)
1 cup plain yogurt

1 cup water
¼ cup honey
2 tablespoons almond oil or vegetable oil
1½ teaspoons unsulphured blackstrap molasses
1 egg
⅔ cup raw sunflower seed
¼ cup raw sesame seed
2 to 3 tablespoons rolled oats

Preheat oven to 350°F. Generously grease 9 × 5-inch loaf pan. Combine whole wheat flour, soy flour, bran flakes, wheat cereal, dry milk, baking soda and powder in large bowl. Combine yogurt and water in another bowl. Add honey, oil, molasses and egg to yogurt mixture and beat with fork. Make well in center of dry ingredients and add yogurt mixture and sunflower and sesame seeds. Stir just until moistened; *do not overmix.* Pour batter into prepared pan. Sprinkle with rolled oats. Bake until tester inserted in center comes out clean, about 55 minutes. Let cool on rack. Serve warm.

To freeze, cover tightly with plastic wrap and aluminum foil. Rewarm slices in 350°F oven for 10 to 15 minutes; rewarm loaf 25 minutes.

Whole Wheat Cornmeal Bread

This bread freezes well.

Makes 2 8 × 4-inch loaves

2½ cups sour milk*
2½ cups whole wheat flour
1 cup cornmeal
1 cup golden raisins (optional)

½ cup sugar
½ cup molasses
1½ teaspoons baking soda
1 teaspoon salt

Preheat oven to 375°F. Grease two 8 × 4-inch loaf pans. Combine all ingredients in large bowl and mix thoroughly. Divide evenly between prepared pans. Bake until tester inserted in centers comes out clean, about 30 minutes. Cool loaves slightly before slicing.

*For sour milk, combine 3¼ tablespoons lemon juice with enough milk in measuring cup to equal 2½ cups liquid.

Basic Croissants

These layered rolls can be made over a period of several days, if desired, as there are two stopping places in the basic recipe. The croissants can also be completed in advance and frozen.

Makes 24 croissants

2 envelopes dry yeast
¾ cup warm water (105°F to 115°F)
3¾ cups unbleached all purpose flour
½ cup milk
2 teaspoons sugar
2 teaspoons salt

2 cups (4 sticks) unsalted butter, well chilled and cut into ½-inch pieces

1 egg beaten with 1 tablespoon milk

Combine yeast and water in medium bowl and stir until yeast dissolves. Add ¾ cup flour with milk and sugar and whisk until smooth. Cover bowl with plastic wrap. Let stand in warm area, about 75°F, 1½ to 2 hours to mature. (An oven preheated to lowest setting 1 minute and then turned off works well.) About halfway through rising process, batter will bubble up, then sink down; if preparation is to be discontinued at this point, stir bubbles out of batter and refrigerate up to 24 hours; maturing process will continue.

Combine remaining 3 cups flour with salt in large bowl. Add well-chilled butter and mix, flattening butter pieces slightly between fingertips and working quickly so butter remains firm. (Refrigerate butter mixture if yeast batter is not ready to use.) Pour yeast batter into flour mixture and carefully fold in using large rubber spatula, just moistening flour without breaking up butter pieces; dough will be crumbly.

To fold dough: Turn dough out onto lightly floured surface. Pat dough down and roll into 18 × 12-inch rectangle; if dough is sticky, sprinkle top lightly with flour. Using metal spatula or pastry sheet, fold right ⅓ of dough toward center, then fold left ⅓ over to cover (as for business letter); dough will still be slightly rough. Lift folded dough off work surface, scrape surface clean and sprinkle lightly with flour. Repeat patting, rolling and folding dough 3 more times. (If butter starts to soften and run, immediately wrap dough in plastic and freeze 10 to 15 minutes; butter pieces must remain layered throughout dough to ensure flaky pastry.) Wrap in plastic and chill at least 45 minutes (or up to 24 hours).

To shape croissants: Pat dough into rough rectangle. Cut in half lengthwise through center, then crosswise into thirds, forming 6 equal pieces. Return 5 pieces to refrigerator. Roll remaining piece out on well-floured surface into 5½ × 14-inch rectangle. Using pastry cutter or long sharp knife, divide dough in half crosswise to form two 5½ × 7-inch pieces. Cut each piece diagonally to form a total of 4 triangles. Using rolling pin, gently roll across shortest side of 1 triangle, until dough measures 7 inches across. Gently roll from longest side to point until dough measures 8 inches across. Holding point of triangle with one hand, loosely roll dough up from base to point with the other hand. Transfer croissants tip side down to ungreased rimmed baking sheet. Curve both ends down slightly, forming crescent. Repeat with remaining dough.

Brush croissants with egg mixture. Set aside, uncovered, in warm area (70°F to 75°F) and let rise until doubled in volume, about 1 to 2 hours; reglaze with egg mixture once during rising.

To bake: Position rack in center of oven and preheat to 450°F. Reglaze croissants with egg mixture. Bake until puffed and golden brown, about 12 to 15 minutes. Let cool on rack at least 10 minutes before serving. (Croissants can be cooled completely, wrapped airtight and frozen. Reheat unthawed croissants in 375°F oven for 10 minutes.)

Danish Pastry

All of the filled pastries can be refrigerated for three days or frozen, prior to baking.

Makes about 100 miniature pastries

1½ cups (3 sticks) unsalted butter, room temperature
⅓ cup all purpose flour

¼ cup warm water (105°F to 115°F)
2 envelopes active dry yeast or 2 cakes compressed
1 tablespoon sugar
1 cup milk
¼ cup sugar
1 egg, beaten

3½ to 4 cups all purpose flour

Fillings (see following recipes)

1 egg
1 tablespoon water
Sugar Glaze (optional; see following recipe)

Streusel Topping (see following recipe)

Cream butter with ⅓ cup flour until well blended. Cover and chill until firm enough to roll, about 30 to 45 minutes.

Combine water, yeast and 1 tablespoon sugar in large mixing bowl and let stand to proof. Add milk, sugar and egg and blend well. Gradually add 3½ cups flour, beating well after each addition until dough is smooth and glossy (dough should not be sticky; add more flour if necessary). Turn out onto lightly floured board. Shape into ball. Dust with flour and roll into 16-inch square.

Turn butter mixture out onto another floured board. Roll and shape into 8 × 16-inch rectangle (butter should roll out like a pie crust; if it does not, return to refrigerator and chill). Place on half of dough. Turn other half of dough over butter and press edges together to seal.

Using rolling pin, roll or lightly pound dough into rectangle ½ inch thick. Fold ⅓ of dough to center and fold remaining third over top, making 3 layers. Turn folded dough toward you so one of narrow ends faces front. Roll out again,

🍎 Croissant Tips

As easy as croissants are to make in advance, a few simple guidelines will make them even better.

- Dough must remain chilled as you work with it. Place in freezer for 10 to 15 minutes (or in refrigerator about 30 minutes) if butter begins to soften.
- When rolling out dough, lift frequently and sprinkle the work surface with flour to prevent sticking.
- Use a flat pastry brush to remove excess flour from dough after it has been rolled out. A feather pastry brush is ideal for applying egg glaze.

fold and turn. Repeat for a total of 3 times. Wrap and refrigerate 30 to 60 minutes (or freeze 10 to 20 minutes, but do not freeze solidly). Repeat rolling, folding and turning 3 more times. Wrap and let rest in refrigerator 30 to 60 minutes (or freeze 10 to 20 minutes).

The dough is now ready for shaping and filling. Form and fill as desired, using directions and recipes that follow.

Butter baking sheets. Place filled pastry on prepared sheets, cover lightly with towel and refrigerate 1 to 2 hours.

About 15 minutes before baking, preheat oven to 400°F. Beat egg with water and brush lightly over pastries. Bake 5 minutes. Reduce oven temperature to 350°F and continue baking until pastries are lightly browned, about 10 minutes. Cool slightly, then brush with Sugar Glaze if desired. Let cool completely.

To serve, preheat oven to 200°F to 300°F. Place pastries without touching on baking sheet. Set in oven, turn off heat and let warm through.

Unbaked filled pastries can be refrigerated for 3 days and baked as needed, or they can be frozen. If frozen, bake without thawing at 425°F until just lightly browned, about 8 to 10 minutes.

Fillings

Nut Paste
- 1 egg
- 1 cup nuts, ground
- ½ cup firmly packed brown sugar
- Pinch of cinnamon

Beat egg in small bowl. Add remaining ingredients and beat to smooth paste.

Apricot or Prune Filling
- 1 cup diced dried apricots or prunes
- 1 cup apricot nectar or prune juice
- ½ cup sugar

Combine fruit and liquid. Cover and simmer until fruit is tender and liquid is thickened, about 20 minutes. Add sugar and stir until dissolved.

Cheese Filling
- ½ pound farmer's cheese
- 2 to 4 tablespoons sugar
- 1 egg yolk
- 1 teaspoon vanilla
- 1 teaspoon grated lemon peel
- Currants or light raisins (optional)

Beat together cheese, sugar, yolk and vanilla in small bowl. Add remaining ingredients and blend well.

Sugar Glaze

1 cup sifted powdered sugar	1½ teaspoons melted butter
1 tablespoon milk	Several drops of vanilla

Blend all ingredients in small bowl.

Streusel Topping

½ cup sugar	Dash of cinnamon
6 tablespoons flour	Chopped nuts (optional)
¼ cup (½ stick) butter, cut into pieces	

Using fingertips, combine all ingredients in small mixing bowl.

Crescents: Roll pastry ⅛ inch thick. Cut into long strips 5 inches wide. Cut strips into triangles 2 inches wide at base. Place about 1 teaspoon filling at base of triangle and roll; twist ends and form a crescent. Place on baking sheet so point of triangle is on bottom to prevent opening while baking.

Envelopes: Roll pastry ⅛ inch thick. Cut into 2- to 3-inch squares. Place about 1 teaspoon filling in center of each. Fold opposite corners of dough over filling, overlapping slightly. Pinch tightly to avoid opening during baking.

Cockscombs or Bearclaws: Dust working surface with granulated sugar. Roll pastry into strip 6 inches wide and ⅛ inch thick. Spread with thin layer of Nut Paste filling. Fold one lengthwise edge of dough ⅓ of way over filling. Fold again. Repeat with opposite edge to make strip 2 inches wide. Gently roll lengthwise to flatten slightly. Fold in half lengthwise. Cut into slices ¾ inch wide. Make 4 or 5 small slits along one side of each slice. Place pastries on buttered baking sheet, curving slices slightly to spread the slits.

Figure Eights or Pretzels: Roll dough into rectangle ¼ inch thick. Cut into strips ¼ to ½ inch wide. Twist each strip so it looks like rope. Cut into pieces 10 inches long. Shape into figure eights or pretzels and transfer to baking sheet. Brush with egg wash and sprinkle generously with sugar before baking.

Elephant Ears: Dust working surface with granulated sugar. Roll pastry into rectangle 4 inches wide and ⅛ inch thick. Spread with Nut Paste filling. Fold one lengthwise edge of dough ⅓ of way over filling. Fold again. Repeat with opposite edge to make strip 2 inches wide. Gently roll lengthwise to flatten slightly. Fold in half lengthwise. Cut into slices ¾ inch wide. Place on prepared baking sheet and flatten slightly.

Cinnamon Pinwheels with Streusel Topping: Roll pastry into rectangle ⅛ inch thick and 4 to 5 inches wide. Brush with beaten egg and dust with cinnamon-sugar. Sprinkle with rum-plumped currants, pressing lightly into dough with rolling pin. Roll tightly like jelly roll. Brush seam with remaining egg to seal. Cut roll into slices ⅓ to ½ inch thick. Place cut side down on prepared baking sheet, pressing slices slightly with palm of hand. Sprinkle with Streusel Topping. Or roll and slice as above, placing heaping teaspoon of cherry preserves on each pinwheel. If using preserves, drizzle tops of pinwheels with light corn syrup before baking to prevent burning.

Moussaka

Red Cooked Anise Beef (top),
Spicy Malaysian Lamb

Feuilletés of Pears Bourdaloue

Danish Pastry

Flaming Plum Pudding